RHS

Get Growing

Brimming with creative inspiration, how-to projects, and useful information to enrich your everyday life, Quarto Knows is a favorite destination for those pursuing their interests and passions. Visit our site and dig deeper with our books into your area of interest: Quarto Creates, Quarto Cooks, Quarto Homes, Quarto Lives, Quarto Drives, Quarto Explores, Quarto Gifts, or Quarto Kids.

RHS Get Growing

Author: Holly Farrell

First published in Great Britain in 2020 by Frances Lincoln, an imprint of The Quarto Group.
The Old Brewery, 6 Blundell Street, London N7 9BH

Published in association with the Royal Horticultural Society

© 2020 Quarto Publishing plc

ISBN: 978-0-7112-5107-6
A CIP record of this book is available from the British Library
Manufactured in Hong Kong

RHS Publisher: Rae Spencer-Jones
RHS Consultant Editor: Simon Maughan
RHS Head of Editorial: Chris Young

Conceived, designed and produced by
The Bright Press, an imprint of The Quarto Group.
The Old Brewery, 6 Blundell Street
London N7 9BH
United Kingdom
(0)20 7700 6700
www.QuartoKnows.com

Publisher: James Evans
Art Director: Katherine Radcliffe
Managing Editor: Jacqui Sayers
Senior Editor: Caroline Elliker
Designer: Clare Barber
Illustrator: See Creatures

The Royal Horticultural Society is the UK's leading gardening charity dedicated to advancing horticulture and promoting good gardening. Its charitable work includes providing expert advice and information, training the next generation of gardeners, creating hands-on opportunities for children to grow plants and conducting research into plants, pests and environmental issues affecting gardeners.

For more information visit www.rhs.org.uk or call 0845 130 4646.

RHS

Get Growing

A family guide to gardening indoors and out

HOLLY FARRELL

F

FRANCES
LINCOLN

Contents

Introduction

Through the eyes of a child, a garden can be so much more than the sum of its parts. Where an adult sees lawns, beds and borders, a child sees a rainforest, a crocodile-infested swamp, the Wild West or a fairy-tale castle. Creating a more colourful, interesting, inspirational and tasty garden space will only further encourage children to play outside and to learn the basic fundamentals behind growing plants – and it's easy to do.

Growing plants is the best way to reconnect with nature and the wild world around us, and to foster a love of and respect for the environment. Learning to garden also offers many opportunities to encourage other educational aspects – whether it's counting out seeds, learning about the science of plant growth, reading plant labels or drawing the flowers – and when in muddy wellies, not shiny school shoes, the lessons tend to go unnoticed!

Gardens are a place of inspiration and relaxation for children – with an easel and an ever-changing flower border on hand, they could be the next Claude Monet, or they might prefer to simply lie and be at the back of the border, like Harry Potter did at 4 Privet Drive. They could discover a love of nature, and spend all day following the antics of the birds and bugs in the garden, or they could be the next top chef, growing and cooking their own food. Even if they are only old enough to push a few seeds into the soil and spill a watering can over a plant, there is still much to be gained from being outside, growing and learning together.

Gardening as a family is a chance to reconnect, not just with nature but with each other. The fascination of watching a bee collecting nectar, the anticipation of pulling up a home-grown carrot, the delight in a line of seeds germinating; these things can all be shared across the generations. Gardening is fun: start today and grow not just plants, but hearts and minds as well.

How to use this book

The best thing about gardening is that it takes very little investment in time or money to get started – and it doesn't even need a garden! The basic, fundamental act of growing plants is something that can be done anywhere and on any scale; from a collection of pots on a windowsill to full-scale allotments and community gardening, any and all opportunities for your family to get growing are covered in this book.

The first chapters cover the basics of gardening; principles that apply to all types of plants such as watering, sowing seeds and planting trees. The following chapters then go into more specific details and give some inspiration about what to grow, from fruit and veggies to herbs and flowers for cutting and wildlife. Refer to both for all the information you'll need to start growing.

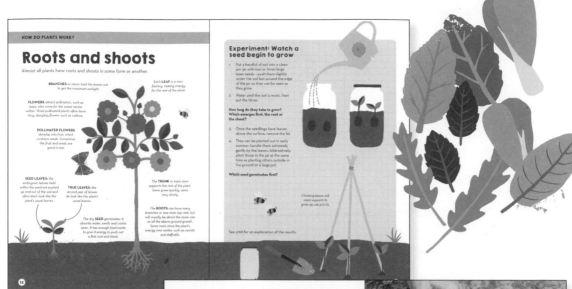

Throughout all the chapters are experiments and projects that help to bring the ideas alive – from turning a white flower red (not magic, but science!) to growing a willow den and making your own fruit squash – and the final chapter has some ideas for garden activities for the different seasons as well as seasonal gardening tasks. A Glossary (see pp170–171) helps with any unknown terms, and there are ideas of where to go next on your gardening adventure in the Further Resources section (see p172).

Where can you grow?

It really is possible to grow plants anywhere, and not having a garden needn't mean not being able to grow. It's always best to get growing gradually, anyway: start with a couple of plants on a windowsill and add to and expand the garden over time, rather than rushing into a big project that then becomes overwhelming. Gardening is all about patience, and enjoying the process of growing and nurturing as well as the fruits of your labours.

This chapter details all the places you could start, and grow, your garden, from a windowsill to an allotment, from containers to beds and borders. There are pages on how to assess your space's growing potential, with some experiments to find out what kind of soil you have, and how much sunshine and rain the garden gets. Plants will grow anywhere, it's just a case of choosing the right plants for the right places.

How does your garden grow?

The first thing to do when starting gardening is to look at how much growing space you have and think about what kind of garden will be possible for your family. Even a tiny patch outside a front door can grow a wealth of plants. Is there open ground, or could some raised beds and containers be put over hard surfaces? Could plants be trained up walls or fences? Don't be put off even if there is no available outside space – a few houseplants can turn indoors into a green oasis to admire.

The next step is to work out how much sunlight the growing area will get, as different plants thrive in different light levels. It's always best to work with nature and grow the best plants for the space you have; for example, trying to grow a sun-loving plant in a shady spot will always end in disappointment.

Use a compass to discover which direction the garden area faces. South-facing gardens get the most sun; north-facing the least. East- and west-facing gardens both get sun, but walls and trees can also cast long shadows as the sun moves throughout the day.

Experiment: Shadow tracking

To work out how much sun the growing space gets, take it in turns to track shadows throughout the day.

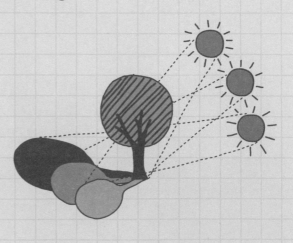

1. Take a large piece of paper and draw an outline of the garden area, marking key features such as trees and patios.

2. Use different coloured pens or pencils to mark the areas in shade at least three times through the day (e.g. after breakfast, lunch and dinner).

3. The results will give a good indication of which spaces get the most sun and which get the most shade.

Remember, there will be more sun in summer and longer shadows in winter.

Experiment: Rain shadows

Buildings, fences and trees can also cast rain shadows - areas of ground that, although outside, don't get much rain falling on them.

After a rain shower, go into the garden and have a look at the ground.

Where is it still dry?

Bear this in mind when planting, as any plants put into those areas will need more watering than the areas where rain falls unhindered.

Growing in the ground

Having some open ground in which to grow generally offers the most opportunities for gardening, but consider (before digging up the lawn) what the garden needs to be used for. Does it need a football pitch or space for a paddling pool?

If everyone can get outside and enjoy the garden in different ways that is what matters, and there are many ways to introduce changes that don't affect the end use. For example, what about allowing the grass to grow longer in places, and letting more wildflowers grow in it? The bees and other wildlife will appreciate the extra nectar, and it shouldn't affect any play. Remember, what is needed from the garden will change over time, and so it, too, can evolve with small, gradual changes that can be just as exciting as introducing big new features, or planting up new borders.

Soil type

Other than light levels (see p12), soil type is the main factor that will affect which plants will thrive. Soil can be sticky clay that bakes hard in dry summers and is prone to waterlogging in winter. It could be dry and sandy soil that drains water away well in winter but needs a lot more watering in summer. Or it could be somewhere in between. Clay helps to hold on to more nutrients, making the soil more fertile, but sand helps with drainage. Each soil type supports different types of plants.

Experiment: Can you make a soil sausage?

To find out where your garden is on the clay to sand scale, take a small scoop of soil from a few places around the garden and mix them all together. Wet it slightly, then take a small handful.

First, roll it into a ball. If it feels gritty and doesn't hold well, the soil is sandy. If it holds in a ball it has some clay.

Next, try rolling it into a sausage shape. If this is possible there is a greater proportion of clay in the soil. If the sausage can be bent into a ring, it is heavy clay.

Experiment: Test the soil's acidity

Another great experiment is to find out whether the soil is acidic or alkaline (or neutral). Most plants grow best in a neutral to slightly acidic soil, but extremes of acidity or alkalinity can make growing difficult. Purchase a pH testing kit from a garden centre or online and follow the pack instructions.

For a more detailed analysis of the soil, RHS members can send a sample to the soil science laboratory for testing (see p172).

How to improve the soil

The ideal soil is in the middle of both the clay–sand scale and the pH (acid/alkaline) scale. Don't despair if the soil is at one extreme or the other, as all soils can be easily improved over time. The best way to do this is to add plenty of compost or well-rotted manure every year (see pp50–51 for advice on buying compost). Give it a sniff – good-quality compost and well-rotted manure shouldn't smell bad!

There is increasing evidence that it is best to leave the soil to its own devices, allowing worms and other soil creatures to incorporate a layer of compost put on the surface every year, rather than carrying out a lot of digging. This allows the complicated soil structure and ecosystem to continue undisturbed, and saves a lot of work for the gardeners – a win-win situation.

However, when creating a new area of garden, some digging can be beneficial. Lawns especially can lead to the soil beneath becoming very compacted, so turning the soil over and digging in plenty of compost before planting can help aerate it and improve the drainage.

Making a new border

The terms beds and borders are often used interchangeably by gardeners, but both mean an area of ground that houses a selection of plants, as opposed to lawn or paving. Typically, borders have something behind them, such as a hedge or wall, and are longer and thinner than a bed, which can be isolated in the middle of a lawn (sometimes called an island bed). Borders also typically contain longer-term plantings of shrubs and perennials, whereas beds are used for bedding (annual) plants. However, it's not necessary to get the terminology right to have a beautifully planted garden!

To create a new bed or border in the ground:

- Mark out its edges with a hose or a line of sand.

- Use a spade to cut out around the edges. If needed, slice under the grass to remove it (pile up the grass, upside down, and it will rot down into soil again).

- Dig over the area thoroughly, removing any roots and large stones.

- Spread a thick layer of compost over the top. Turn and mix this in with the soil using a garden fork or spade.

- Walk (do a penguin shuffle) over the whole area to start to level it out, then finish levelling with a rake.

- Plant or sow with seeds (see pp52–55).

Note that gardens of newly built houses often have very thin soil and lots of rubble beneath, so more compost and extra topsoil may be needed once the rubble has been removed.

Growing in raised beds

What is a raised bed?

A raised bed is a box of soil or compost in which plants can be grown.

When are raised beds useful?

Raised beds can create a space for growing where there is no ground. They offer more opportunities for growing large plants and trees than pots and other containers. They can be used for permanent plantings of trees and perennials, or for annuals such as a vegetable or cut flower patch. They can also help in gardens with poor soil: by having a raised bed over the top, it is possible to grow a greater variety of plants.

Raised beds are useful where accessibility is difficult – they bring the soil level to waist height or higher, meaning it's possible to garden from a wheelchair or just with less bending.

Finally, raised beds offer a number of advantages over growing in the soil. Their soil/compost warms up faster in spring than open ground, offering a head start to seed-sowing of vegetables or flowers and allowing plants to come back into growth sooner. When built so that the entire area can be reached from either or one side of the bed there is then no need to tread on the soil or compost within the bed, so compaction never becomes a problem.

How do I grow plants in raised beds?

Sow, plant and maintain the beds as for any other area of the garden. Top up the compost level annually.

Building raised beds

🌱 Raised beds are straightforward to construct from timber, and they are fun to clad or paint if you like. You can buy pre-cut kits in various forms and sizes, or a bit of DIY can create one quickly.

🌱 Make sure that the timber has not been treated with chemicals that could leach into the bed and then potentially the plants (especially if they are edible crops). This is particularly true of some old railway sleepers, which used to be treated with creosote. Either use untreated hardwood or treated wood that is certified acceptable to use for organic growing by the Soil Association.

🌱 When designing the beds, consider access and the volume of soil that will be needed to fill them. A width of 1.5m is ideal as this can be reached without having to tread on the bed itself. If the bed is sitting on top of a hard surface rather than soil, line the base and sides with something such as a polypropene membrane, fixing it to the sides with tacks or staples. This will allow excess water to drain away and help to contain the soil/compost. Lining the sides only of beds sitting on soil will help to extend the life of untreated timber but does introduce plastic to the garden. See p51 for advice on buying compost.

Growing in containers

A pot of herbs on a windowsill is a great way to get started: everything is contained in a small space and there is only one plant's needs to attend to. That single pot can quickly grow to a large collection, and even when there is the opportunity to grow outside, there is always a place for containers.

Advantages of containers

Pots and other containers can be tailor-made to perfectly suit each plant's needs. For example, they are ideal for growing blueberries in areas with neutral or alkaline soil, as the blueberries can be planted in a pot of the acidic compost they need, instead of having to try and change the pH of the garden soil.

Many plants – and even small trees – can be grown in containers. New plants more suitable for pots are being brought onto the market every year.

It is easy to move and then change the content of pots, allowing for seasonal displays and also the growing of more tender plants that can be moved under cover for winter.

Everyone can grow what they want in their own pot – so that the whole family has their own mini-garden.

What to be careful of when growing in containers

Make sure that the container has suitable drainage, and add drainage holes if not. If there is no way to add drainage holes, use the container as an outside cover pot in which to hide a less attractive (plastic) pot that houses the actual plant.

Be aware that pots and containers require more regular watering than plants in the ground – the smaller the pot, the faster it is likely to dry out.

Use pots and containers to grow:

- A few small, pretty, edible or scented plants to put onto an outside table.

- Herbs outside the back door for easy picking when it's raining.

- Seasonal displays of spring bulbs or summer annuals.

- Tender plants such as succulents, or those that need winter protection such as lemon and olive trees.

- Plants that have different soil or drainage requirements, for example alpine plants, acid-lovers or water-lovers such as wasabi and watercress.

Growing up

When short of ground space, consider growing in another dimension.

Window boxes

The simplest form of using the vertical space is more about growing down rather than up. Window boxes or hanging baskets planted with trailing plants allow for some relatively large plants compared with the size of the root space. Just be sure to keep them well-watered and fertilised and a few annual plants will flower for months.

Climbers and trained trees

Climbing shrubs, perhaps planted in the space of a single lifted paving slab at the foot of a wall, can easily cover the face of a building if well cared for. Some climbers require wires or trellises to scramble up or to be trained along (such as roses, wisteria and clematis), others will cling to the wall themselves (such as Virginia creeper, ivy and climbing hydrangeas). Climbing plants help to insulate houses and can make a plain wall a lot more appealing.

Some trees and shrubs, particularly fruit trees, are easily trained against a wall or fence and need relatively little root space to give a good harvest of fruit or display of flowers. Apple trees will even do well on a north-facing wall. Look for plants that are labelled 'dwarfing' or that have had had their young branches already trained, and ask specialist fruit growers about the best trees and training methods to use (see pp96–97 and Further Resources, p172).

Living walls

Living – or green – walls are systems of pockets into which plants are placed, either with or without soil, and which grow to ultimately fill in the whole space with foliage. Often used on the sides of large new buildings, they are also achievable at home using proprietary pocket systems or a home-made rig of guttering and watering pipes. The watering of these walls needs careful attention and they are more limited in the types of plants that can be used, but they are a good option for introducing greenery to a wall or fence.

Green roofs

Flat and sloping roofs – of buildings varying in size from wheelie bin stores to apartment blocks – can be used to grow alpine plants, herbs and grasses. Refer to specialist books and websites for advice on constructing a green roof (see Further Resources, p172).

RIGHT *A mix of species in a green wall adds textural interest as well as different colours.*

Growing inside

Houseplants offer the chance to grow a range of exciting plants that wouldn't survive outside in a temperate climate, such as those that originate from jungles and deserts.

Why not grow...

- A herb garden on the kitchen windowsill?

- Chillies, lemongrass, ginger and turmeric? All will grow easily in a warm, sunny spot indoors.

- Cacti and succulents? A 'shelfie'-worthy collection of plants.

- Jungle plants in a steamy bathroom? They help to reduce condensation, too.

- Hanging pots of trailing plants? These are perfect above the kitchen table or over the banisters.

- Trailing plants on bookshelves?

- Leafy palms in the living room?

- Fragrant jasmine in the conservatory?

Things to be aware of

Light levels

Indoor light levels are considerably lower than outside, and artificial light is not a good substitute. Keep windows clean and put plants in an appropriate spot. In summer, giving plants a stint outside gives them a health boost. Rotate plants regularly, as they can start to lean towards the light.

Draughts

Cold draughts from windows and doors, and hot air rising from radiators and fires, can cause leaves to brown at the edges. Keep plants out of these areas where possible.

Watering

Houseplants need regular checks and watering, but they also benefit from a daily mist with a spray bottle to increase the humidity around their leaves (the air in centrally heated homes can be quite dry).

Dust

Dust and limescale can settle on the plants' leaves, which reduces the amount of light getting to the leaves even more. Give plants a regular shower and/or wipe the leaves with a soft cloth to keep them clean.

Other options for getting growing

If there is simply no space – or no more space – at home to make a garden, don't despair. There are still plenty of other opportunities to get growing.

School gardens

An increasing number of schools are using part of their grounds to grow fruit and vegetables, either to be used for school meals and home economics classes or to be sold by the pupils to raise funds. If your school doesn't have a garden, ask to start one.

Allotments

Many towns, cities and villages have at least one allotment site. Check the local council website to find the nearest, then contact them for vacancies. Having an allotment has become increasingly popular in recent years, and some sites have long waiting lists, but it's worth asking if existing tenants are looking to share a plot or need some help tending their allotment.

Sharing with neighbours

There may be space to garden closer to home. Ask if any neighbours would either like help with their garden or would be willing to share it, particularly the elderly who may not be able to maintain their gardens as well as they used to. Gardening in this way is beneficial as it strengthens community ties, and older gardeners can be a font of information that they are more than happy to pass on.

Community gardens

Search on the internet or look on noticeboards for a local gardening club. They may be able to help find a garden share or have a community garden space or orchard that needs volunteer gardeners. Often these spaces are in public areas, and having well-tended gardens and beds around the city or town helps to improve everybody's lives (there is evidence that the greener a local area, the lower the levels of anti-social behaviour and vandalism). If there isn't anything along these lines, why not start something?

LEFT *Allotments offer plenty of space for growing and a community of like-minded plot holders.*

Gardens for tricky situations

Not everyone can have a south-facing garden with fertile, well-draining soil, but that doesn't mean that not everyone can have a fantastic garden. Make the most of the situation that nature has presented.

A shady garden with large trees

There are many plants that thrive in shady, dry soil beneath trees. Look to woodland plants for inspiration – plant bulbs for spring colour before the leaves come out on the trees, and consider adding some plants along the lines of forest gardening, where different layers of trees, shrubs and ground cover can all be beautiful and even productive (see Further Resources, p172).

A concrete courtyard

Make the most of the microclimate (the specific conditions created by the space) – courtyards often have higher temperatures than an open garden would, so can grow plants that would otherwise get frosted such as tree ferns, citrus trees and olives. Use collections of containers, grouped to give a sense of flow and unity, to divide up the space, and consider some planters around the walls in which to grow climbers.

A long, narrow garden

This is the perfect opportunity to divide up a space into garden 'rooms', different areas that have different functions. Create a sense of mystery by having the path meander down the garden, so the end cannot be seen from the house. Use large shrubs, small trees, trellises with climbing plants or hedges to divide up the garden so that all the family has a space to plant what they want.

Steep slopes

A slope can be terraced to give more planting space, or the whole bank can be planted with low-maintenance trees, perennials and groundcover plants.

Dry, stony soil

Many Mediterranean plants thrive in these conditions – plant lavender, rosemary and thyme, for example, for a fragrant and beautiful garden. Visit gardens with gravel gardens for inspiration, e.g. RHS Garden Hyde Hall.

Wet, boggy soil

Plant water- and bog-loving plants such as the enormous-leaved gunnera, irises and arum lilies. Consider adding a pond to make the most of the site.

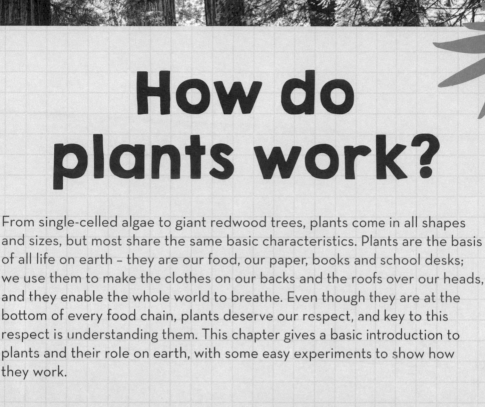

How do plants work?

From single-celled algae to giant redwood trees, plants come in all shapes and sizes, but most share the same basic characteristics. Plants are the basis of all life on earth – they are our food, our paper, books and school desks; we use them to make the clothes on our backs and the roofs over our heads, and they enable the whole world to breathe. Even though they are at the bottom of every food chain, plants deserve our respect, and key to this respect is understanding them. This chapter gives a basic introduction to plants and their role on earth, with some easy experiments to show how they work.

Roots and shoots

Almost all plants have roots and shoots in some form or another.

BRANCHES or stems hold the leaves out to get the maximum sunlight.

Each **LEAF** is a mini-factory, making energy for the rest of the plant.

FLOWERS attract pollinators, such as bees, who come for the sweet nectar within. Wind-pollinated plants often have long, dangling flowers such as catkins.

POLLINATED FLOWERS develop into fruit, which contains seeds. Sometimes the fruit and seeds are good to eat.

SEED LEAVES: the embryonic leaves held within the seed are pushed up and out of the soil and often don't look like the plant's usual leaves.

TRUE LEAVES: the second pair of leaves do look like the plant's usual leaves.

The **TRUNK** or main stem supports the rest of the plant. Some grow quickly, some very slowly.

The **ROOTS** can have many branches or one main tap root, but will usually be about the same size as all the above-ground growth. Some roots store the plant's energy over winter, such as carrots and daffodils.

The dry **SEED** germinates: it absorbs water, swells and cracks open. It has enough food inside to give it energy to push out a first root and shoot.

Experiment: Watch a seed begin to grow

1. Put a handful of soil into a clean jam jar with two or three large bean seeds – push them slightly under the soil but around the edge of the jar so they can be seen as they grow.

2. Water until the soil is moist, then put the lid on.

How long do they take to grow? Which emerges first, the root or the shoot?

3. Once the seedlings have leaves above the surface, remove the lid.

4. They can be planted out in early summer: handle them extremely gently by the leaves. Alternatively, plant those in the jar at the same time as planting others outside in the ground or a large pot.

Which seed germinates first?

Climbing beans will need supports to grow up, see pp72–73.

See p168 for an explanation of the results.

Making food from light

Plants are at the bottom of the food chain – that is, everything eats them and they don't eat anything else (except carnivorous plants – see pp148–149) – and because of this it is tempting to view them as less important than animals. Actually, they are the foundation of all life on earth. Without plants, the rest of the world would topple and fail.

So, where do plants get their energy from?

Well, plants can do something no animal can: make their own food. This doesn't mean they're putting on aprons and baking their own bread, it means they can turn a few basic chemicals into food (energy). They do this through a process called photosynthesis, which means 'making food from light':

CARBON DIOXIDE + WATER (WITH SUNLIGHT AND CHLOROPHYLL) → SUGAR + OXYGEN

Every green part of a plant is used for photosynthesis, and inside each green cell is a mini-factory using light to turn carbon dioxide and water into sugar (glucose) and oxygen. Photosynthesis only happens in the green parts of plants because the cells need a green substance called chlorophyll to make the process work.

Photosynthesis means that not only are plants able to make food from sunlight and thin air, but they are also recycling carbon dioxide into fresh oxygen for us to breathe. Plants can help in the fight against climate change: too high levels of carbon dioxide in the atmosphere are leading to rising temperatures around the globe. Plants help to balance the gases in our earth's atmosphere, so the more plants there are, the better it is for the world.

CO_2

Experiment: Cress heads

Use fast-growing cress seeds to prove how essential light is to a plant's growth.

1. Carefully wash out three empty egg shells.

2. Fill each one with a little compost, water until the compost is very damp, then sprinkle cress seeds over the top.

3. Draw a face on the shells with a marker pen and put them in egg cups or old egg boxes to keep them upright.

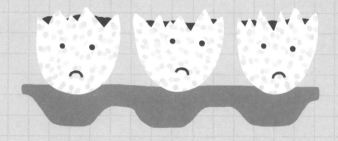

4. Put one shell on a sunny windowsill, one in a dark cupboard and one in a gloomy but still light place.

Which cress head grows the best hair?

See p168 for an explanation of the results.

The water chain

All plants need water, and most suck it up from the soil through their roots, but how do they get the water to their topmost leaves?

The process is called transpiration, and it's a little like how humans sweat. Water evaporates through tiny holes in the plant's leaves. The hotter, drier or windier the weather, the faster the water in the leaves evaporates.

As one tiny bead of water is pulled out of the leaf into the air, it pulls another into the leaf, and that pulls another and that pulls another, and so on and so forth all the way into the branch and then down a tube in the trunk called the xylem, then into the roots in one long, unbroken chain of water. Transpiration helps to cool the plant, and also to pull up nutrients from the soil, dissolved in the water.

Plants losing water from their leaves is why the air in a greenhouse is always more humid than that outside, or the air below a tree is cooler than in the sun, or why mist rises from forests – it's the water in the air. Many litres of water every hour evaporate from a large tree or field of crops.

Experiment: Turn a white flower red

Watch how flowers still pull up water,
even when they have been cut off the plant.

1. Take a white flower with a stem of about
    20–30cm (8–12in) and some leaves, making
    sure that the end has been cut neatly from
    the plant. If it is a bought cut flower, cut off
    the bottom 10cm (4in) or so of stem, as this
    will have dried out and broken the water
    chain. Leafy sticks of celery with their ends
    trimmed can also be used.

2. Put the flower stem in a glass or vase of
    water and add some food colouring to
    the water (it needs quite a lot – the
    water should be quite dark with
    colour). Red is best, but you could
    use any colouring. Put one flower in
    just water.

**It will take a little while, but what happens to
the flowers?**

Why not try several vases each with a different
colour? You could even split a stem in half
lengthways with a sharp knife and put each
half of the stem in a different coloured water.

See p168 for an explanation of the results.

Energy storage

Just like a bear eating lots ready to hibernate or a squirrel burying nuts for its winter food stores, plants that live through the winter need to store energy so they are ready to grow again in the warm spring weather. Bulbous plants, such as daffodils, snowdrops and tulips, store their energy in an enlarged root – the bulb – from which they can regenerate new roots and leaves every year.

Growing bulbs in a vase

By growing bulbs in a glass vase with no soil it is possible to see the roots and shoots emerging:

- In autumn, put some flower bulbs (e.g. daffodils or tulips) in the fridge or plant outside in a small pot, as they need to experience the cold in order to flower.

- In late winter, dig up and wash off planted bulbs or get them out of the fridge.

- Put the bulbs on top of a layer of gravel or glass pebbles in the base of a vase.

- Maintain a layer of water as deep as the pebbles and put in a warm place then watch them start to grow and flower.

Another example of plants storing energy in their roots are vegetables. Many common vegetables are actually just the means of biennial plants storing energy and if left in the ground they would go on to flower and set seed (then die) the following year. Carrots, parsnips, beetroot, swede and celeriac are all examples of plants storing energy in their roots. They store the energy initially as sugars, but over time (and especially after it has been harvested) those sugars turn to starch, which is why a home-grown carrot eaten straight from the garden will always taste sweeter than a shop-bought one.

Experiment: Carrot top planting

To show that the roots of plants store energy, try planting a leafless carrot top.

1. Take the top section of a carrot (the bit that is usually chopped off and thrown away) and push it down into a small pot of damp soil or multipurpose compost. Leave the very top exposed, but make sure the cut surface is slightly under the soil.

2. Leave it on a warm, sunny windowsill, making sure that the soil/compost stays damp, for a few days.

What happens to the carrot top?

See p168 for an explanation of the results.

Nature's recycling

Eventually plants will die, or parts of them die every autumn; their old leaves and stems rot down, eventually turning back into soil and providing essential nutrients for the plants still growing. In nature, the process of turning old plants back into soil is carried out by millions of organisms, from insects such as beetles and woodlice to microscopic creatures and fungi.

Some of the heroes of the composting cycle are worms. As they burrow through the soil they mix it all together and carry plant debris from the surface to under the soil to be eaten up and broken down. A wormery can be a great way to compost kitchen scraps (see Further Resources, p172), and it's easy to make a temporary one to see how the worms work.

Experiment: Make a wormery

1. Take a large jar or bottle with a metal or plastic lid and make sure it is completely clean. Carefully punch small holes in the lid: it's essential that air can get in, but the worms can't get out.

2. Add layers of soil and sand to create a stripy effect, spraying or sprinkling each layer with water until it is damp.

3. Add some vegetable peelings (avoid onions and citrus fruits) to the top.

4. Find some worms in the garden. Carefully put them into the bottle/jar and seal the lid.

5. Keep the wormery in a dark place and check on it every day.

What is happening to the layers of soil and sand?
Can you see the tunnels the worms are making in the soil?
What has happened to the veg peelings?

6. Make sure the soil remains damp, and return the worms to the garden after a week or so.

See p168 for an explanation of the results.

Gardeners can recycle the plant waste in their garden – and kitchen peelings too – in a compost heap. For more advice on how to create and maintain a compost heap in the garden, see Further Resources (p172).

Ecosystems

An ecosystem is all living things and the land/water in a particular place, and different ecosystems are found all over the world. The Amazon rainforest is an ecosystem, which is very different to the ecosystem of a British seashore, and both of those contrast with a back garden in a city.

All the components within an ecosystem are in a delicate balance. Disrupt the ecosystem (for example, through climate change, deforestation, pollution or invasive species) and the balance – and the ecosystem – can be lost forever.

Within an ecosystem, everything has a role to play. Plants are crucial as they create the energy on which everything else will feed (see also pp34–35). For example, in a savannah ecosystem the plants (grasses) make the food. Herbivores such as zebras and antelopes eat the grass, and the energy is passed on to them. Carnivores such as lions eat the zebras and the energy continues up the food chain. The lions eventually die of old age and are decomposed by bacteria and insects, rotting back into the ground where the nutrients feed the grass: and so it continues to cycle around.

However, the whole world is also one giant ecosystem in which plants also help cycle the gases that make up our air and the water. To show how plants are the lungs of the earth a scientist sealed himself in an airtight box with plants: he breathed out carbon dioxide and the plants recycled it into oxygen as he lived in there for 48 hours (don't try this at home).

Experiment: Make a terrarium

A terrarium is a mini ecosystem; a plant or collection of plants in a sealed container. The plants don't die because they continuously recycle the air and water inside; there are some more than 40 years old and still thriving. To make your own:

Take an old jar and make sure it is completely clean.

1. Put a layer of sterile gravel or glass pebbles at the bottom, then a layer of multipurpose compost and into which put a shade- and moisture-loving plant or two (miniature ferns are ideal).

2. Make sure the compost is damp all the way through, but not sodden, then seal the jar.

3. Watch the plant(s) continue to live even though no more water or air is added.

For longer-term terrariums, a layer of activated charcoal between the gravel and compost layers helps keep the water pure – this can be found in aqua and garden centres. A layer of moss over the top of the soil makes the whole thing look greener, too.

The building blocks of gardening

No matter what kind of garden you want to grow – large or small, jungle or herb garden – the basics are all the same. This chapter will tell you how to go about buying plants, sowing seeds and planting, and how to look after your garden once you've created it.

How to identify a plant

Learning the names of plants isn't necessary (though it is fascinating) but understanding the kinds of conditions plants need to thrive is the first step to becoming a successful gardener.

Be a garden detective

HOSTA

The leaves can give a big clue as to where a plant likes to grow. Large or wide leaves (e.g. hosta) indicate it prefers growing in shady, damp areas, whereas thin, narrow leaves are typically seen on plants that grow in dry, sunny places (to minimise water loss from their leaves e.g. lavender). Sticky, oily, hairy or fleshy leaves, such as those on cacti and succulents, all also suggest a plant prefers full sun and free-draining soil.

Then look at the leaf and flower size, shape and colour. Use these to look up the plant, either in a book or using an identification app. Otherwise, ask someone you know who likes to garden, staff at a plant nursery, on social media, or the RHS Advisory Service (see Further Resources, p172).

Why do plants have Latin names?

All known plants have a botanical Latin name (there are, no doubt, many still to be discovered and named), and this can be a bit off-putting. It's much easier to use the common name and say 'aren't those bluebells pretty?' rather than 'aren't those *Hyacinthoides non-scripta* pretty?', and common names are fine for day-to-day gardening.

ENGLISH BLUEBELL

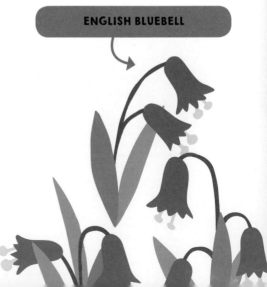

However, the problem with common names is that different common names are used for the same plant, and the same common name is used for different plants. The bluebell, for example, could be an English bluebell, *Hyacinthoides non-scripta* (which is also called crake feet, fairy flower and squill, among other things), or it could be the Italian bluebell, *Hyacinthoides italica*. It could even be a completely different plant, *Mertensia virginica*. In fact, the RHS has 43 different plants in its database, all associated with the name 'bluebell'!

Botanical Latin names allows gardeners and scientists from across the world to talk to each other about plants and be sure that they are talking about the same thing.

Where to get plants

Plants are readily available in many outlets, including supermarkets, garden centres, plant nurseries or online plant shops, local plant sales and seed swaps (often in aid of charity) and boot fairs.

How to buy plants

The cheapest way to get a lot of plants is to grow them from seed, and certain plants such as quick-growing vegetables and annuals will only be available as seeds. Others can be bought as trays of young plants (plug plants), such as strawberries, vegetables, annuals and some herbacous perennials.

Larger plants such as herbs, shrubs, ornamental trees and houseplants are available all year round from most plant retailers. Fruit bushes and trees are best bought in winter, as they are generally available 'bare-root', which means they are sold without a pot or compost around their roots. They need to be planted straight away but are much more economical than buying potted bushes/trees in spring and summer.

Quick checks

It's easy to get carried away in a garden centre, so before going shopping do some research and make a list.

- Some retailers will put out greenhouse-grown plants for sale long before they would actually survive outside, so be sure it's the right time of year to be buying the plants. For example, climbing bean seedlings could be on sale in March but would be killed by a frost if planted outside before early summer.

- When buying seeds, check they are within their 'sow-by' date.

- Plants should look green and healthy (short and stocky with plenty of new shoots), with no signs of pest or disease.

- Check that their roots fill the pot (not a few roots and a lot of loose compost) but aren't wound tightly round in it (rootbound) – tip the plant out of the pot briefly to make sure.

- Is the pot recyclable? Many plants are now being supplied in taupe, rather than un-recyclable black, plastic pots. Check if the pot is recyclable, or whether there is an alternative to plastic pots available, such as coir pots or wrapping the rootball in paper.

- Finally, be sure that the retailer has a no-quibbles return policy, especially if buying plants online.

What else will I need?

Most garden tools can be improvised, so there's no need to make a big outlay on equipment at the beginning. When buying tools, invest in the best quality you can afford so that they last as long as possible. Some manufacturers also offer warranties and repair services. Otherwise, buy second-hand equipment, which is often easy to find in charity shops and boot fairs, or borrow from or share tools with neighbours or friends.

Basic kit

This is the basic kit needed to get started:

A PAIR OF SECATEURS
for cutting back and pruning (for non-woody plants, strong scissors will do to start with).

GARDEN TWINE *for tying in climbing plants.*

A **HAND FORK** *for weeding and lifting root veg.*

A **TROWEL** *for digging planting holes and scooping compost.*

PLANT LABELS – *get reusable ones or make them (e.g. from cut up old plastic milk bottles).*

CANES, HAZEL STAKES *or other supports for climbing plants and wooden stakes for newly planted trees.*

A **GARDEN FORK** *for turning in compost and aerating the soil (not essential, can be done with a spade).*

A **RAKE** *for levelling and removing stones from the soil surface (before sowing seeds).*

A **HOE** *for quick removal of annual weeds from the soil surface in summertime.*

A **SPADE** *for digging the soil.*

A **WATERING CAN** *with a detachable rose attachment for the spout.*

Buying compost and topsoil

Always get the best quality multipurpose compost that's within budget. Organic and peat-free are good environmental choices, but the peat-free substitutes (such as coir) also have an environmental impact. Some nurseries now offer loose compost in reusable bags to reduce plastic packaging. Local green-waste compost from the council is inexpensive and can be used for most garden purposes, though check it can be used for potting plants.

When buying topsoil, again get the best affordable quality but ensure that it has been screened and sterilised, otherwise there is a risk of importing really problematic weeds such as Japanese knotweed, horsetail and bindweed into the garden.

Sowing seeds

Seeds are a fun and relatively inexpensive means of adding new plants to the garden. Just remember – each seed is a potential new plant, so only sow what you need with a few extras for contingencies.

Seed-sowing basics

- Water the soil or compost before sowing the seeds so they are not washed away.

- Cover the seeds with twice their height in compost – for example a 1cm (³⁄₈in) bean seed needs burying 2cm (³⁄₄in) below the surface; a tiny lettuce seed should only be covered with a thin layer.

- To sow in a straight line (drill sowing), scratch out a shallow trench or press a bamboo cane or short stick into the surface, sprinkle the seeds along it then gently cover with soil.

- To sow seeds with larger gaps between the plants (station sowing), use a pencil to make small holes for each seed.

- Check the seed packet for more detailed information.

Sowing direct in the ground and raised beds

- This saves time, but plants can be more easily lost to slugs, snails and other pests like mice that may eat the seeds.

- Ensure the soil is weed-free and any stones have been raked off.

- Water the area, then sow in lines or individual spots, as required.

Sowing direct in pots and other containers

- Fill the container with multipurpose compost, removing or crumbling any large lumps in the top layer.

- Water thoroughly, then sow using a pencil to make the holes or a short stick to make a drill.

Sowing in small pots to grow on

Get a head start by sowing inside then planting out little plants once it's warm enough.

Ideally, use home-made biodegradable pots to house young seedlings that can then be planted out in their pots. Make pots out of paper using a proprietary paper pot maker, cut out the individual parts of a cardboard egg box, or use loo paper inner tubes stacked in a tray. Alternatively, reuse or recycle plastic pots (e.g. yoghurt pots) or tins and carefully add drainage holes using a skewer.

Fill with multipurpose compost, water and then put a couple of seeds in each small pot. Once they have germinated, remove the weaker seedlings. Keep on a sunny, warm windowsill until the roots are filling the pot, then plant into a bigger pot or plant out into their final position.

To make a larger box for growing plants on even longer inside, cut up old cardboard boxes and make them into small square pots using paper masking tape to fasten the sides together.

Planting in pots and in the ground

Water plants well before planting out.

Planting in pots

Any plant can be grown in a pot, even dwarf trees, but always give them as big a pot as possible.

Make sure large drainage holes are covered with broken pieces of pot, large stones or something that will similarly allow excess water to drain away but prevent the compost from being washed into the hole or out of the pot entirely.

Multipurpose compost will be fine for most plants grown in pots, though trees and shrubs will benefit from a soil-based compost. Partially fill the pot with compost, firm it down, then put the plant (out of its existing pot) on top. If the plant is sitting a little low in the pot, add more compost underneath. Once the plant is at the correct level, fill in around the edges with compost, firming the rootball in well.

The compost level should be around 2–3cm (³/₄– 1¹/₄in) below the rim of the pot. This prevents the compost washing over the edge when watering. Give it a good soak of water.

Planting in the ground

Dig the hole bigger than the rootball of the plant, and loosen up the soil around the base of the hole with a garden fork.

Put the plant in, adding more soil underneath if necessary so that where the roots turn into stems is level with the soil. Rotate it so its best side is facing out. Gently tease out the roots of larger shrubs and trees where possible.

Backfill around the rootball, firming it in well. If the soil is poor, mix a bit of compost with the backfill soil.

Give it a soak of water, and add a mulch of compost, ensuring it doesn't touch the stems.

Support trees with a stake, fastened to the tree with a cushioned tie.

Planting out young plants

Always handle small plants by a leaf and the rootball, never the delicate stem.

Watering your plants

Watering is the most basic and necessary task you can perform for your plants, but it's one that often causes a lot of anxiety in a new gardener. Follow these simple rules for watering success.

Does it need watering?

The only way to know if the soil or compost around a plant is dry is to feel it. It might look wet on top, perhaps after a short rain shower, but underneath it can still be dusty and dry; or it may look dry on top but still be soggy underneath. Stick your finger in the soil around the roots:

• If it feels soggy, it won't need water today.

• If it feels dusty, water it straight away.

• If it feels damp or moist that's perfect, but remember to check again tomorrow.

There are a couple of exceptions to these general rules, such as succulents and carnivorous plants. Check p136 and p148 for more information.

Water in the morning or evening if possible, directing the water at the roots not the foliage. Water a little at a time and let the water sink in before adding more, so it stays around the plants' roots rather than running off, and to avoid washing away soil/compost.

Experiment: How much rain actually ends up in the pot?

After rain it's tempting to think that outdoor potted plants won't need watering but it's surprising how little falls onto the pot. If you're curious...

1. Get a bucket and a full watering can with a rose attachment.

2. Pour the water over the bucket, trying to make it fall as rain would (the higher you are the better).

3. When the can is empty, pour the water in the bucket back in it.

How much water actually fell in the bucket?

See p168 for an explanation of the results.

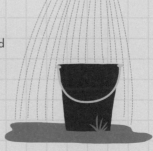

What to use

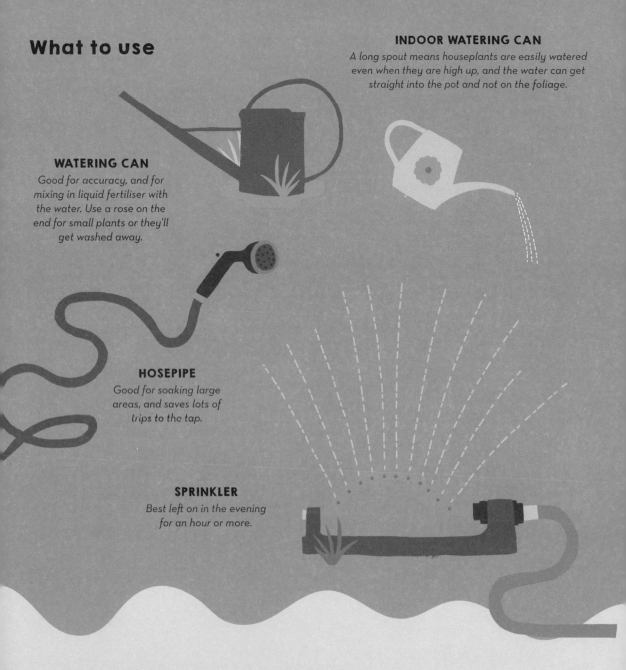

INDOOR WATERING CAN
A long spout means houseplants are easily watered even when they are high up, and the water can get straight into the pot and not on the foliage.

WATERING CAN
Good for accuracy, and for mixing in liquid fertiliser with the water. Use a rose on the end for small plants or they'll get washed away.

HOSEPIPE
Good for soaking large areas, and saves lots of trips to the tap.

SPRINKLER
Best left on in the evening for an hour or more.

Re-using water

Collecting rainwater in a water butt is a brilliant way to avoid wasting water and it's better for the plants than tap water. It is also possible to save water by collecting old washing-up or bathwater ('grey water') and putting that on the plants, especially when only environmentally friendly soaps have been used. However, it's best not to use it on edible plants, and don't use it all the time to avoid soap levels building up in the soil.

Going on holiday?

No-one wants to come back from holiday to find wilted or dead plants where their garden once was. The best way to keep things properly watered while you're away is to ask a friend or neighbour to look after things for you. If that's not possible, collect pots together and put them in a shady place to reduce their need for water and give everything a really good soak before you go.

Slow-water bottles

A slow-water bottle can be a good trick, both for going away and to reduce the need to water. Cut the base off a large plastic drinks bottle and pierce a few small holes in the lid using a hammer and nail or drill. Bury the upended bottle next to the plant so it's stable, and fill with water. The water will drain slowly from the holes in the lid and keep the soil moist.

Feeding your plants

Just as we need vitamins and minerals to keep us healthy, plants also need extra nutrients to grow well, resist attacks from pests and diseases, and ensure they flower and fruit to their full potential.

Plants growing in the ground and raised beds

Keeping a healthy soil is really all that's needed. Add a layer (mulch) of good-quality compost and/or well-rotted manure every year in late winter or early spring. Make sure the mulch isn't piled up around the plant stems or trunk. Over the year the worms will incorporate the mulch into the soil, which will add nutrients and help with drainage.

Plants in containers

Plants growing in containers quickly use up the available nutrients. There are two options for feeding container plants:

1. Controlled-release fertiliser (often called 'slow-release')

These are capsules of fertiliser that are buried in the pot and dissolve over time. Add to the pot in spring, following the label instructions.

2. Liquid fertiliser

A concentrated formula of nutrients that is added to watering. This gives a more instant boost to growth, but needs to be repeated regularly. Follow the instructions on the label.

Which fertiliser?

Most plants will be happy with an all-purpose or general fertiliser; there is not usually any need for plant-specific feeds. Liquid seaweed is a good organic option.

Home-made fertiliser

Collect a bucketful of nettles or comfrey (*Symphytum officinale*) leaves and stems, squashing them down. Cover with water and leave to steep for 3–4 days. Drain off the liquid and water onto the plants.

The liquid run-off from wormeries (see p41) also makes a brilliant fertiliser when diluted at a ratio of 1:10 with water.

COMFREY LEAVES

Cultivating a healthy garden

No matter how well a garden is nurtured, there will inevitably be some hiccups along the way. Accepting these is all part of the learning curve for becoming a gardener.

Your garden as an ecosystem

Treating a garden as an ecosystem and a chance to observe nature in all its glory is preferable to viewing a garden as a collection of prize plants and all the rest of nature as potential enemies. As with all ecosystems, the key is in keeping a balance. Make space for creatures that are the gardener's friends, such as birds, frogs, toads and hedgehogs and in turn they will help by keeping the aphid, slug and snail populations under control. Plant flowers that will attract hoverflies and ladybirds, and they and their larvae will also happily predate on aphids.

Healthy plants are also more likely to be able to withstand a low level of pests or disease, and healthy plants start with a healthy soil. Add compost or well-rotted manure every year, and try not to disturb the soil and its own delicate balance of microscopic creatures by digging or walking on it as little as possible.

Avoid over-feeding plants as this can create a lot of lush green foliage that is more likely to attract bugs that feed on the sap.

Keep weeds under control in beds and borders, as they can create humidity around plants (which can foster fungal diseases), hide slugs and snails, and use up available water and nutrients.

LEFT *Encourage bird life – they will eat aphids and insects that can damage your garden, reducing your need to use pesticides.*

When growing vegetables and other annual plants, avoid planting the same type of plant in the same place every year. Rotating different plants around the space gives pests and diseases less of a chance to build up over time.

Dealing with diseases

Keeping a regular eye on plants and removing pests or diseased leaves as soon as they are seen will often avoid any further problems. However, tolerating a low level of infestation is necessary to give something for garden predators (e.g. ladybirds) to feed upon.

Where a plant has a disease, removing old leaves from around the base and cutting out diseased stems (and burning where possible) can break the cycle of re-infection and help prevent the spread.

Keep tools clean and sharp, and always wash with detergent after dealing with a diseased plant.

When dealing with a pest or disease, use chemicals only as a last resort and always follow the label instructions.

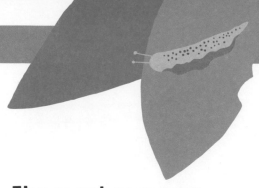

The most common pests

Slugs and snails

Easily identifiable and most active in the early morning and evening. Check under pots and in nooks and crannies during the day. Relocating slugs and snails is the most humane way to deal with them, but they do have a homing instinct.

Aphids

Also known as greenfly and blackfly (whitefly are not technically an aphid but have a similar effect on plants), they cluster around the lush shoots and flowers at the plant's tips. Look for them under leaves and spot their sticky excretions on the leaf surfaces as well. Remove by squashing them – washing them off doesn't work as they will just climb back up again.

Caterpillars

Can cause little damage in low numbers, but can also decimate a plant. However, there would be no butterflies or moths if gardeners squashed all the caterpillars. Tolerate a low level of infestation – again, birds will help to keep levels down – or pick them off and relocate to weed plants or wildflowers in a nearby park or wild hedgerow.

The most common diseases

Mildews

The most common plant diseases, causing a whitish layer of fungus on leaves. Ensure plants are kept healthy with correct watering and feeding, and that there is not too much humidity around the leaves. Remove infected parts as soon as they are seen.

Blight

Generally affecting tomato and potato plants, it causes grey, brown and black blotches on leaves and stems and spreads rapidly. More likely to infect plants in humid, damp conditions. Remove infected parts as soon as they are seen and whole plants if necessary to prevent further spread.

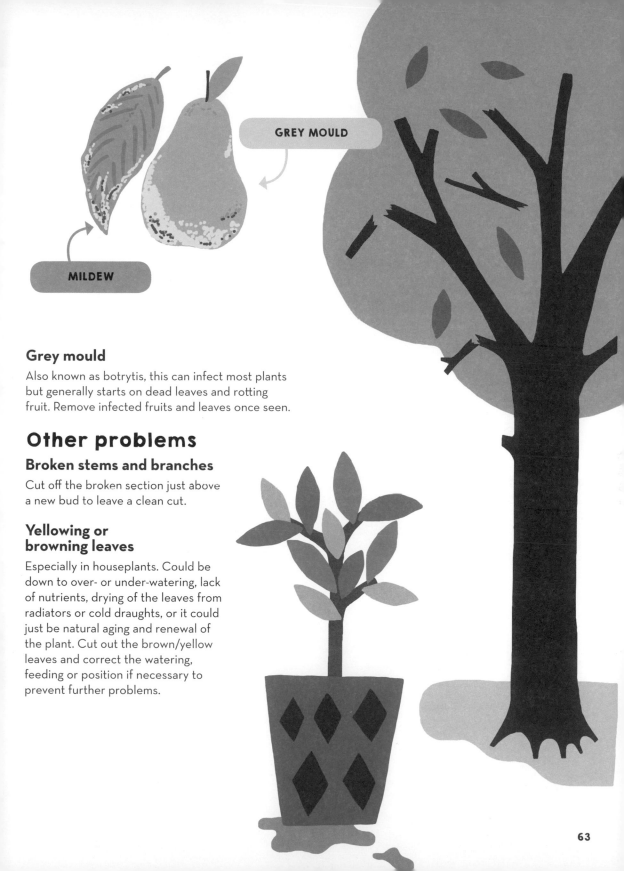

GREY MOULD

MILDEW

Grey mould

Also known as botrytis, this can infect most plants but generally starts on dead leaves and rotting fruit. Remove infected fruits and leaves once seen.

Other problems

Broken stems and branches

Cut off the broken section just above a new bud to leave a clean cut.

Yellowing or browning leaves

Especially in houseplants. Could be down to over- or under-watering, lack of nutrients, drying of the leaves from radiators or cold draughts, or it could just be natural aging and renewal of the plant. Cut out the brown/yellow leaves and correct the watering, feeding or position if necessary to prevent further problems.

Weeds and weeding

Nature abhors a vacuum, and will quickly fill the spaces between young plants with weeds. A little weeding on a regular basis (for example a few minutes when you get home, or while picking fruit and veg) is the best way to keep them under control and prevent it from becoming a chore.

Weeds are simply a plant growing in the wrong place, and while some can be more invasive than others, a lot of weeds are actually considered to be wildflowers in other circumstances and are loved by wildlife, especially insects. Having a wilder patch of the garden where they are allowed to grow freely can help to attract helpful wildlife. Some weeds are also edible, though be sure of the identification by using guides or apps before you start munching.

Annual weeds

These weeds grow from seeds, flower and set seed again within a single season – some, such as hairy bittercress, many times over spring and summer – so the adage 'one year's seed, seven years' weeds' applies to these plants. Avoiding letting weeds flower and setting seed goes a long way to keeping the weed levels down.

They are also the easiest types of weeds to just pull out by hand or hoe off, especially when small, and are fine to put into the compost if they haven't made seeds.

EXAMPLES: fat hen, cleavers (goosegrass), chickweed, grass.

Perennial weeds

More problematic, as they tend to root deeply (e.g. dandelions, horsetail and dock) or widely (e.g. ground elder, bindweed, couch grass, buttercups and stinging nettles). Dig out using a handfork or spade, removing all the roots, as most will regrow from any part of the root left in the ground. They also spread by seed, so remove any flower spikes as an interim measure. Spread dug-up weeds in the sun until completely shrivelled and dead before composting, or burn to be on the safe side.

RIGHT *A weed is simply a plant in the wrong place; and many are actually pretty wildflowers.*

Get growing... veg

Growing your own vegetables is a great way to learn about where our food comes from, what it takes to produce it and how tasty vegetables can be. In this chapter, you will find out about fun vegetables to grow for garden snacking such as peas and cherry tomatoes, art projects to do with salad leaves and pumpkins, corn on the cob and more.

Vegetables prefer a sunny, sheltered position with good, rich soil, and with planning, a lot can be grown in a small space. Refer to the general advice on seed-sowing and plant maintenance in The Building Blocks of Gardening (pp44–65), along with the specific details for each vegetable in this chapter.

Each type of vegetable has a few recommended varieties to try but there are many more, each different and all with something to recommend them (colour, size or taste) so it comes down to personal preference and experimenting with the best choices for your garden and family. However, look out for those varieties that have an Award of Garden Merit (AGM), as these have been tested by the RHS and were found to have performed well in a typical garden setting.

Growing peas and broad beans

Eating peas straight from the pod is a highlight of a summer garden, and extracting beans from their furry pods makes broad beans fun to grow.

Varieties to try

- **Traditional peas** – 'Early Onward', 'Kelvedon Wonder'
- **Sugar snap peas and mangetout** – 'Oregon Sugar Pod', 'Sugar Ann'
- **Broad beans** – 'Aquadulce Claudia', dwarf 'The Sutton'.

Sow

Peas, sugarsnaps, mangetout and tall broad beans benefit from some support – push a line of twiggy sticks along the edge of the line of seeds for peas to scramble through, and tie broad beans loosely to canes. Sugarsnaps and mangetout can be grown like peas, but tall varieties can be grown up a wigwam (see p72). Loosely tie them to canes as they won't twine in the same way as climbing beans.

To grow peas in a pot, push a bundle of twiggy sticks into the middle of a large pot and sow the seeds around the outside edge. Dwarf broad beans can be grown without support in pots or rows. Sow in spring, spacing the seeds about 7cm (2¾in) apart for peas and 20cm (8in) apart for broad beans.

Grow

Pinch out the tips of the plants once they are about 10cm (4in) high to encourage bushy growth.

Pick

Once the peas are ready, the pods will be fat and firm. Split open and enjoy raw, or cook.

Broad beans can also be felt through the pods; pick young for a less mealy-tasting bean, and cook before eating.

The shoots (peas only) and flowers are edible, but picking the flowers means fewer pods. Regular picking will extend the plants' pod production for as long as possible. Sow two or more batches of seeds a few weeks apart to stagger the harvests.

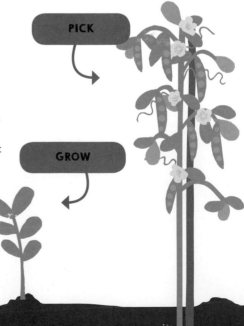

PICK

GROW

SOW

🌱 Project: Saving seeds

Collecting seeds from home-grown plants saves money and is an environmentally friendly way of getting seeds for sowing the following spring. Seeds saved from plant varieties labelled as 'F1' on the packet may not produce such good plants the following year as the original variety has already been heavily manipulated by the plant breeders.

1. In autumn, leave a few pods on the plant to dry and go hard.

2. Pick the pods, take the peas or beans out from the pod and put them in a paper bag.

3. Tie up the top and hang it somewhere cool and dry to allow the peas or beans to dry completely.

4. Store the peas or beans in a jar or tin in a cool place until the following spring.

Growing carrots

Will they be long and thin or short and round? Forked or twisted? It's impossible to know until the carrots are pulled from the soil – each one a delicious surprise.

Varieties to try

- For sandy soil or raised beds of compost, the 'Nantes' cultivars or a packet of mixed colour seeds are a good choice

- For pots, clay or stony soil, choose short or round cultivars such as 'Parmex' or 'Paris Market Atlas'

- 'Flyaway' and 'Resistafly' have some resistance to carrot fly.

Sow

Sow in March, and then again in April for successive harvests.

Sprinkle the seeds about 1cm (3/8in) apart in a line, or over the surface of a pot. Cover lightly.

Grow

Keep the area free of weeds. The plants can be covered with a tunnel of fine mesh to keep out carrot fly, which will burrow into the carrots, leaving them inedible, but growing them surrounded by other strong-smelling vegetables and herbs (e.g. basil, spring onions, chives) can help put the bugs off the scent.

Pick

Pull up every other carrot once the roots are large enough to eat, to allow the rest more space to grow. Carrots will reach their full size in three to four months – pull up a test one to see if it's big enough. Use the leaves in salads or in place of basil to make pesto.

SOW

GROW

PICK

Did you know...

... carrots weren't always orange? In fact, the original carrots were yellow, white or purple and were mostly only eaten for their leaves and seeds. Orange carrots were bred in Holland around 500 years ago, and are associated with the House of Orange, the royal dynasty.

... the idea that eating carrots can help you see in the dark was a piece of Second World War propaganda by the British? They spread the story that the Royal Air Force ate lots of carrots in order to disguise the fact that the pilots were actually using new radar technology to help with night-time bombing raids. Carrots are good for eyesight, though, as they are rich in Vitamin A.

Growing climbing beans

Growing climbing runner and French beans up a wigwam of canes or a trellis saves space.

Varieties to try

- **Runner beans** – 'Scarlet Emperor', 'White Lady'
- **French beans** – 'Cobra', 'Blue Lake', 'Cosse Violette', 'Kingston Gold'
- **Borlotti beans** – 'Lingua di Fuoco 2'.

Sow and plant

Make a wigwam of eight long bamboo or hazel poles, pushing each firmly into the ground and tying them together securely at the top. To grow in a large pot, use four or six poles.

In mid-spring, sow in small pots, two seeds to a pot. Grow on a sunny windowsill, planting out into their final position at the base of each cane in early summer once all risk of frost has passed.

Alternatively, sow direct into soil or compost in late spring, putting two seeds to each cane.

Climbing beans like a rich soil, so when sowing or planting in the ground mix a good trowelful of compost into the soil at the base of each pole.

Remove the weaker seedling so that each pole has just one plant growing up it.

Grow

Help young plants to twist themselves onto the poles by gently curling them around the cane or tying them on loosely with garden twine.

The plants will die back in autumn – cut them down and compost them.

Pick

Regular picking of young pods will keep them producing all summer long.

GROW

PICK

SOW

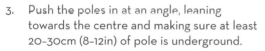 Project: Make a living summer wigwam

Make the wigwam extra-large and it creates a shaded den, perfect for summer picnics and play.

1. Choose a sunny site: it would be fine to do this on the lawn – just dig out a small planting hole from the grass, it will recover quickly in autumn.

2. Space the poles (hazel will be stronger than bamboo) in a large circle – big enough to have a decent seating area in the middle, but small enough that you will be able to tie them together at the tops. Leave a section of the circle clear for the door.

3. Push the poles in at an angle, leaning towards the centre and making sure at least 20–30cm (8–12in) of pole is underground.

4. Tie the poles together at the top and around halfway up so the whole structure is sturdy. Extra string lines will help the plants spread between the poles and cover the whole structure.

5. Add a couple of nasturtium seeds or plants to the beans for colourful (edible) flowers (see also p114).

Growing sweetcorn

The sugars in sweetcorn start to turn to starch immediately as they are picked, so rush the cobs to the kitchen or barbeque straight away.

Varieties to try

Sweetcorn needs a long, hot summer to mature well, so varieties that are quick to mature are the best choices in an uncertain climate. Look for:

• 'Swift F1'

• 'Earlibird'

• 'Lark'

• For popping corn (where the whole cob is microwaved), try the multicoloured 'Fiesta'.

Sow

Start seeds indoors on a sunny windowsill. Old loo paper tubes are ideal, as sweetcorn needs a deep space for its roots to develop.

Sow in mid-spring, then plant out in early summer into a sunny spot protected from strong winds.

Plant out into blocks or squares of plants, not single rows, as sweetcorn is wind-pollinated and needs to be surrounded by other plants to grow good cobs.

Grow

Keep weeds down by growing other crops such as pumpkins or salad around and beneath the sweetcorn plants.

If necessary, tie each plant loosely to a cane or pole support to prevent them breaking in windy conditions.

Pick

The cobs will be ready to harvest in late summer and autumn when the tassels on their tops have turned brown. Test for ripeness by peeling back the green/brown layers and piercing a kernel with a fingernail – if it oozes milky-white sap it is ready.

Hold the cob firmly and twist and pull it upwards to separate it from the plant.

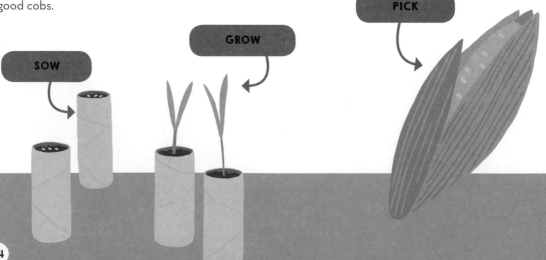

SOW

GROW

PICK

Did you know...

... that there will almost always be an even number of rows of kernels on each cob of sweetcorn? To find a cob with an odd number of rows would be like finding a four-leaved clover – not impossible, but extremely rare.

... sweetcorn is the type of corn (also called maize) that we eat as a vegetable, but other types of corn are also used to make thousands of other products including cornflakes and cornflour, animal feed, biomass for renewable fuels, sweeteners in fizzy drinks, glue, paint and medicines.

Growing salad leaves

Growing a selection of different salad leaves – from dark and spicy to sweet and crunchy – means there will be something everyone will like.

Varieties to try

Many retailers offer packets of mixed varieties, which are a good choice in a small space. To create the salad art opposite, you will need a few packets of individual varieties – try green and red lettuces, rocket, pak choi, sorrel and purple basil.

Sow

Sow direct where they are to grow, sprinkling the seeds in a thin line or sparingly over the top of a pot and covering with a thin layer of compost.

Rather than sowing the whole row at once, sow part rows every two weeks to ensure a good supply over the whole summer and into autumn.

First sowings can be made from mid-spring; the last sowing in late summer.

Grow

Keep well-watered, especially in hot weather when plants can bolt (flower and then make seeds), which results in bitter, tough leaves. Pull out any bolted plants and discard.

Pick

Harvest the oldest leaves (those around the outside) each time, starting when the plant has reached about 5–10cm (2–4in) in height. Always leave a few leaves on the plant.

◐ PROJECT: Salad art

Why not create a living picture by sowing different colours and types of leaves in patterns? Geometric designs, such as squares and stripes, are the most straightforward, but why not try spirals or faces? Sprinkle the pattern over the soil with sand first to help get the seeds in the right place.

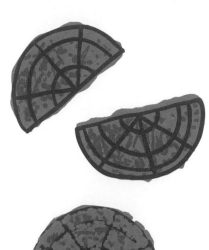

Alternatively, make a globe of salad using hanging baskets. Ambitious gardeners could even try using purple leaves for landmass and green for oceans to create a lettuce earth.

1. Take two hemispherical (half-globe shaped) hanging baskets and a bag of sphagnum moss (available from garden centres or online).

2. Stuff moss into each basket, then wire them together into a globe.

3. Top up the moss by pushing it through the gaps so it is a relatively tight ball.

4. Soak the whole thing in water for ten minutes then stand it over a bucket until the excess has dripped away.

5. Carefully push the rootballs of small lettuce plants into the moss, spaced evenly around the globe (about 10cm/4in, apart).

6. Hang in a sunny spot and water and/or spray daily to keep the moss damp, mixing in some liquid feed regularly.

7. The lettuce will grow to cover the whole ball.

Growing tomatoes

Super-sweet and tastier than shop-bought, home-grown tomatoes are ideal for garden snacking.

Varieties to try

Tomato plants can either be cordons or bushes. Cordons grow tall and need tying in to a cane or pole, bushes don't need any support and are a good choice for hanging baskets and windowboxes.

Select your desired size and shape of tomato – cherry and cherry plum are smallest, then salad and plum varieties, and finally the large beefsteak tomatoes.

Cherry tomatoes are most likely to ripen outside. Good choices include:

• 'Sungold'

• 'Gardener's Delight'

• 'Tumbling Tom'

• 'Sweet Million'.

There are also a number of dwarf varieties, ideal for growing inside on a sunny windowsill, such as 'Red Robin'.

Sow

Although tomatoes are easy to grow from seed, some are also available to buy as young plants, though there will be less choice of variety than by growing from seed.

Sow indoors on a sunny windowsill in small pots from early March, and plant outside in early summer (once all risk of frost has passed).

Grow

Plant in the sunniest spot available, preferably with good air circulation to avoid blight (see p62), either in the ground, a large pot or a growbag. Tomatoes will do well with protection from a greenhouse.

Keep the soil or compost damp and avoid extremes of wet and dry where possible, as irregular watering can cause the tomato skins to split.

GROW

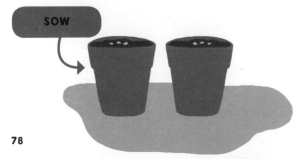

SOW

CUT OFF THE TOP *of the plant once it has three or four fruit trusses and remove the lower leaves to help the fruit ripen.*

Pick

Harvest once the fruits are their final colour by lifting each tomato up so that it cracks from the truss where it bends.

PICK

Is a tomato a fruit or a vegetable?

Garden scientists (called botanists) class tomatoes as fruits because they have seeds and grow from flowering plants. In America, tomatoes are legally classed as vegetables so that they can be taxed (fruits are not) – it was argued in court that tomatoes are more commonly eaten with savoury foods rather than for dessert.

The world's biggest food fight

Every August, 20,000 people squash into the Spanish town of Buñol and throw more than 100 tonnes of ripe tomatoes at each other for an hour. Nobody quite knows how the festival, called La Tomantina, started over 50 years ago, but it now attracts so many tourists that the town only allows people with tickets to enter.

CORDON VARIETIES *need tying into their supports regularly, and side shoots should be removed to leave just one stem of leaves and fruit trusses.*

Growing pumpkins and courgettes

A courgette plant or two can keep a family in fresh vegetables all summer long. And why not try growing an enormous pumpkin for Halloween?

Varieties to try

Courgettes come in long cylinders or spheres, in green or yellow. Choose from trailing varieties (that can also be trained upwards) or more compact bushy plants. Good choices include:

- 'Supremo'
- 'El Greco'
- 'Defender'.

For pumpkins try:

- 'Jack o' Lantern'
- 'Crown Prince' – blue-skinned and tasty
- 'Atlantic Giant' – for huge pumpkins
- Spaghetti squash – with ribbons of yellow flesh.

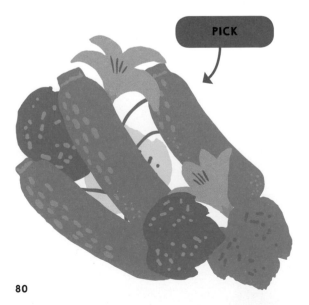

PICK

Sow

Start plants indoors in April. Plant out to a sunny spot in early summer, allowing them plenty of space (refer to the seed packet). Making a shallow dip in the soil or compost and planting in the middle of it helps to concentrate watering around the roots.

Grow

Trailing courgettes can be grown up a trellis or tied gently into a strong cane or pole.

Keep plants well-watered as they can suffer from mildew (see p62) – remove affected parts as soon as they are spotted.

Put developing pumpkins on a flat stone or similar to prevent patches of rot appearing where they are in contact with damp earth.

Pick

Pick courgettes regularly, as they quickly turn into watery marrows if left on the plant. The flowers are also edible – try them stuffed and fried in batter.

Pumpkins are ready to harvest in autumn, when the skin is hard and they sound hollow when tapped. Cut the stalk and put them in a cool, sunny place such as a shed windowsill to mature for two weeks before eating (they can be carved straight away).

PROJECT: Patterned pumpkins

As pumpkins grow, any scratches they get on their skin harden into pale brown scars. By exploiting this it's possible to create faces and patterns on the pumpkin that will still be there when it is harvested. If there's one pumpkin on the plant that you particularly want, why not write your name into it?

1. Being careful not to break the plant's stem, use a marker pen to draw the pattern onto the skin.
2. Ask an adult to carve it carefully into the surface, removing a thin strip of skin for each line.
3. Watch your artwork grow over the coming weeks.

Growing chillies

Chillies come in so many wonderful shapes and colours and add spice to all sorts of dishes.

PRESERVE

Varieties to try

For the biggest choice, buy seeds or plants from a specialist chilli grower online or at plant fairs.

• 'Numex Twilight' has fruits that ripen at different times, so the compact bush is covered in chillies of red, orange, purple and yellow, all at the same time

• 'Hungarian Hot Wax', 'Cayenne' and the mild 'Poblano' are all good choices.

Sow

Chilli seeds need to be sown in late winter in pots that are then put in a heated tray called a propagator. A home-made version could be made by tying a plastic bag over the top of the pots, and putting them on a tray over a radiator. Alternatively buy young plants in spring.

Plant out into large pots or the ground (they will do best in a greenhouse or on a sunny windowsill indoors) in early summer after all risk of frost has passed.

Grow

Pinch out the tips of the young shoots to encourage a bushy plant. Keep well-watered. Plants grown inside or in a greenhouse will benefit from being sprayed (misted) with water every day, as this helps with pollination and preventing pests.

Pick

Chillies are mature (ready to eat) when they are firm to a gentle squeeze. They are ripe when they have reached their final colour. The taste varies widely between these two stages and is entirely down to personal preference.

Preserve

A string of dried chillies is both a useful and pretty thing to have in the kitchen. Simply harvest the ripe chillies and string them onto a piece of cotton by using a sewing needle to thread the cotton through the stalk of the chillies. Hang somewhere warm, dry and with good air circulation – in a sunny windowsill for example – until dry. Break off individual chillies to use as needed.

GROW

Growing potatoes

Although potatoes are relatively inexpensive in the shops, there is a real magic to digging for them in the ground or a pot that makes them worth growing.

Varieties to try

New potatoes are the best ones to grow for flavour, and they are ready for harvest first. Potatoes are grown from special seed potatoes, available from late winter, and new potatoes are sold as 'first earlies'.

- 'International Kidney' or 'Red Duke of York' – try these for their red skin.

- 'Purple Majesty' or 'Violette' – these purple-fleshed potatoes are great for their novelty value and health benefits.

Sow

Seed potatoes bought in late winter should be chitted (given the chance to start growing small green shoots) while it is still too cold for them to be planted outside. Put them in an old egg box and leave on a cool, light windowsill for a few weeks for them to grow dark green shoots.

Plant out the potatoes about 15cm (6in) deep in early spring, allowing two potatoes per 15 litres of space in the pot or bag; or spacing them 30cm (12in) apart in rows.

Grow

Once the shoots appear above the surface, mound up the soil or compost over the top (see opposite for pot or sack growing). This will protect them from frost and encourage more potatoes to grow. Repeat this step twice more. Keep the plants well-watered in dry spells, and cover exposed shoots with a thick layer of newspaper overnight if a frost is forecast.

GROW

SOW

84

Growing in sacks or bins

An easy way to keep mounding up the soil over the top of the growing potato plants is to grow them in large pots, bins or old plastic sacks (e.g. compost sacks). Fill the container about a quarter full then plant two seed potatoes per 15 litre container, pushing them under the surface. Once the shoots appear, add a layer of compost over the top to bring it to half full, and so on, until the compost reaches the top. To harvest, tip out the whole thing and sift out the potatoes.

Potatoes for Christmas

By sowing special seed potatoes in a bin in August, which is then kept in a frost-free but light place, such as a porch, conservatory or greenhouse, it's even possible to harvest fresh new potatoes for your Christmas dinner.

Pick

The potatoes are ready to harvest once the plant starts flowering – around early to mid-summer. Dig the plant up carefully, being sure to get every last potato out. Pull the potatoes off the plant and discard the rest.

PICK

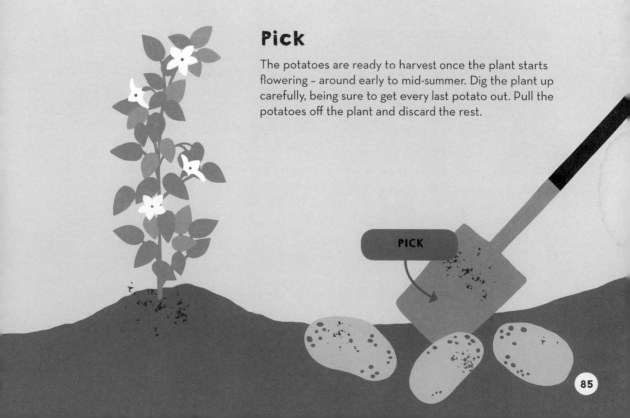

Get growing... fruit

Having a home-grown supply of fruit, especially soft fruit such as raspberries and blueberries, is a real luxury in summer and autumn. Eat it while playing or reading in the garden, or use it to cook up delicious treats (strawberry ice cream or apple pie, perhaps).

Unlike vegetables, which are mostly annual plants sown from seed every year, fruit grows on trees, bushes or perennial plants, so although it is more of an investment in the first year, the plants will continue to produce harvests for many years to come. In fact, the price of a currant bush equates to only a few punnets of the fruit, so it is worthwhile growing your own. See p54 for general guidance on planting and the following pages in this chapter for more specific information about growing each fruit.

Fruit can be grown in its own specific part of the garden, but the trees and bushes also fit in well with a collection of containers or a flower border (so long as they can be accessed for harvesting). The following pages give some ideas for the most popular fruits – strawberries, raspberries, blueberries, apples and more – but there are also many more unusual fruits that can easily be grown in a domestic garden, such as cocktail kiwis, honeyberries and Chilean guava, so seek these out to expand your fruit garden (see Further Resources, p172).

Growing strawberries

Most strawberry plants produce their fruit all at once. Get a few different varieties that do this at various times through early summer to stretch out the harvests. Early season varieties include 'Honeoye', mid-season 'Cambridge Favourite' or 'Marshmello', and a good late-season fruit is 'Malwina'.

Perpetual strawberries such as 'Mara des Bois' produce less fruit at a time, but the plants keep producing all summer. Alpine (or champagne) strawberries are much smaller with a different taste, and also flower and fruit all summer.

Plant

Buy young plants bare-root in autumn to late winter, or potted in trays in early spring.

Plant in pots, hanging baskets or beds, allowing 25–30cm (10–12in) between plants. Make sure the soil/compost is level with where the stems turn into roots. Water well after planting. (See also p150 on how to get more strawberry plants for free.)

Grow

Keep the plants well-watered. Look out for grey mould on leaves or old fruit and remove immediately. Protect the strawberries from birds with a tunnel of netting, pegged down securely at the edges, as the fruit begins to ripen.

Pick

Check the plants every day for ripe fruit. Harvest when they are fully a deep red and smell delicious.

GROW

PLANT

PICK

◉ PROJECT: Make your own strawberry laces

These refined-sugar-free chewy fruit strips can be made with strawberries or any other fruit and keep well in an airtight tin. To make one sheet that can then be cut into strips you will need 500g (1¹/8lb) of washed fruit, with all stalks and leaves removed.

1. Cook the fruit slowly in a saucepan until it becomes a thick, soft puree or pulp.

2. Mix in 75g (2³/4oz) of honey.

3. Cover a baking sheet with greaseproof baking paper and spread the pulp in an even, thin layer over the top.

4. Bake in the oven on its lowest setting (around 60°C) for 12–18 hours. The leather is ready when it is completely dry and peels off the paper.

5. Cut into strips with scissors, roll up and store, or eat!

Growing raspberries

The trick with picking raspberries is to wait until they are perfectly ripe so they are almost falling off the plant.

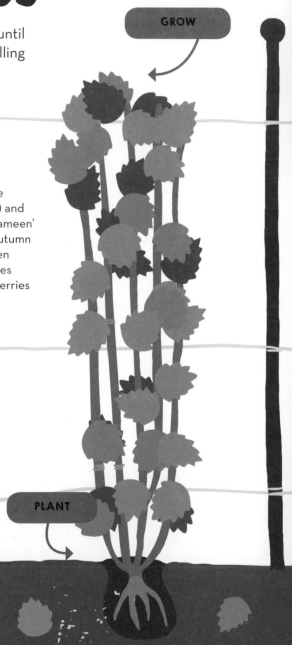

GROW

PLANT

Varieties to try

Raspberries come in summer-fruiting types (which are then divided into early-, mid- and late-season fruiters) and autumn raspberries. Good summer fruits include 'Tulameen' (mid/late), 'Joan J' and any of the 'Glen...' cultivars. 'Autumn Bliss' is a stalwart autumn fruiter. There are also golden and black raspberries, or try some of the hybrid berries (raspberries crossed with other fruits) such as loganberries and tayberries.

Did you know...

... unlike most other fruits, raspberries do not carry on ripening once they have been picked? Only pick the ripest fruit from your plants.

The Raspberry Express

Scotland has the perfect climate for growing raspberries and in the 1950s, fresh berries were taken from Perthshire to London every day on a train called The Raspberry Express. Today, many fruits are imported all year round from other countries, but it's good to eat seasonally and support local farmers.

Plant

Allow 35cm (14in) between plants in a row. Raspberries need some support – a good way to do this is to tie them in to wires on a fence or wall, or stretch wires between two or more posts for a purpose-built raspberry fence. They will still grow well in dappled shade but need rich soil.

Grow

Allow the canes to bend downwards before tying, as this will produce more fruit. Keep well-watered, especially when flowering and fruiting.

Once they have finished fruiting for the year, cut any canes that had fruit on them down to the ground – they won't produce fruit again – this will be some of the summer-fruiting varieties canes and all of the autumn-fruiting ones. Leave new shoots and tie them in, or dig out new shoots that have grown where they are not wanted.

Pick

Raspberries are ripe when they are dark red and pull easily off their central plug.

PICK

Growing currants

Currants are low-maintenance and can produce a lot of fruit from one bush.

Varieties to try

- Blackcurrants – 'Ben Connan' or the slightly more compact 'Ben Sarek'

- Redcurrants – 'Jonkheer van Tets', 'Stanza' and 'Red Lake' are all reliable

- Or try a white or pink currant such as the white 'Versailles Blanche'.

Plant

Allow each bush at least 1.5m (5ft) in all directions and full sun or dappled shade. Unlike most plants, blackcurrants can be planted deeper into the soil, which stimulates the growth of new shoots from the base. Plant so that the crown of each blackcurrant bush is 5–10cm (2–4in) below the soil surface.

⚙ PROJECT: Make your own fruit squash

Home-made cordial is delicious diluted with water for drinking or freezing into ice lollies, and it can be made with whichever berries and/or currants are available. To make 1 litre (1¼ pints) of cordial:

1. Put 1.25kg (2lb 12oz) of washed and de-stalked fruit in a large saucepan (no need to pull the small leafy bits off the currants).

2. Add enough water to cover the base of the pan and simmer gently until the fruit is soft.

3. Mash with a potato masher.

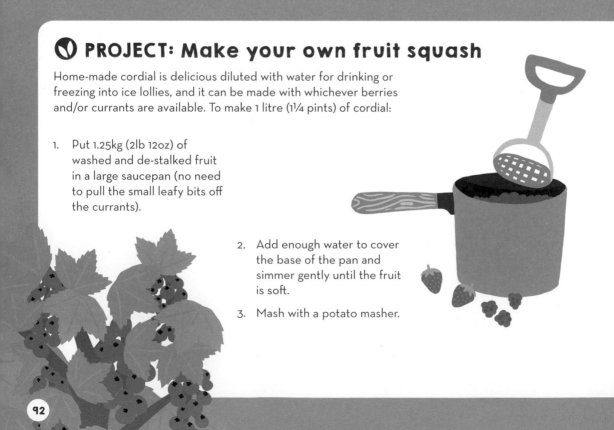

Grow

Prune (cut back) every year to create an open, even shape with no crossing or dead stems.

For blackcurrants, cut out a third of the older stems down to the base every year.

For red- and whitecurrants, take out any dead or crossing stems, then shorten all the new growth to two leaves from the main stem.

Pick

Wait until the currants have turned black or red (creamy white for whitecurrants) then leave for another two to three days to ripen fully. (Net against birds, if necessary). Pick blackcurrants individually (careful – the juice can stain), and pick redcurrants by taking off the whole string of currants, then separating them from the stalk later.

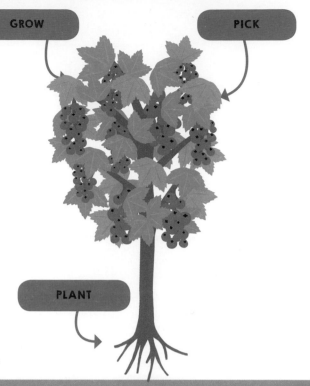

GROW

PICK

PLANT

6. Pour the boiling liquid into clean, sterilised bottles and seal. It will keep for at least three months; once opened, keep it in the fridge.

4. Pour everything from the pan into a jelly bag (a mesh/muslin bag used in preserving) and leave it to drip over a large jug, giving it an occasional very gentle squeeze.

5. Once it has stopped dripping, measure the juice (discard the bag contents or eat with ice cream). Put into a clean pan with 50g (1¾oz) granulated sugar per 100ml (3⅜fl oz) juice. Stir to dissolve the sugar then bring to the boil.

Growing blueberries

Blueberries tend to be one of the more expensive soft fruits, even when in season, and so it is a good investment to grow your own.

Varieties to try

Home-grown berries often have a more intense taste than commercial varieties. Try 'Herbert' or 'Spartan'.

Plant

Blueberries will produce more fruit per bush when planted in pairs or groups rather than singly, because they have more chance of being pollinated. Plant in full sun or dappled shade in acidic soil – create a specific raised bed or collection of pots using a mix of ericaceous (acidic) compost and horticultural grit for better drainage. Allow 1.5m (5ft) between plants in a bed.

Grow

Use rainwater to water the plants, as tap water will make the pH more alkaline again.

Cut one or two older branches back to the ground in winter to keep the plant healthy and a good size.

Pick

Blueberries are ready when they are fully blue and soft. Pull individual berries off the plant gently.

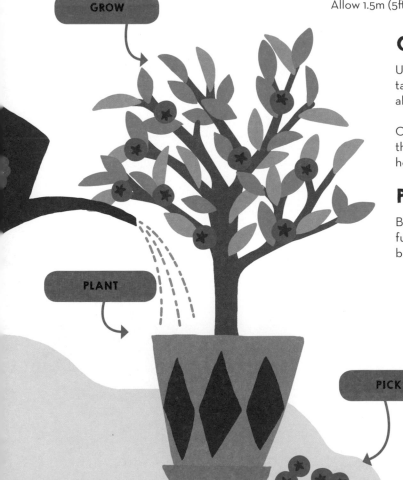

GROW

PLANT

PICK

Did you know...

... blueberries are related to cranberries and bilberries (also known as winberries) and are native to North America, but the biggest growers and exporters of the fruit are now in South America?

Fruit star

Blueberries are also known as star fruit because of the five-pointed star shape on their base (where the flower was). They are stars of the food world too – their natural blue colour is down to a chemical called anthocyanin, which has many health benefits.

Growing apples and pears

The RHS and other open gardens often hold apple days in autumn, when it is possible to taste some of the hundreds of varieties of apples and pears – a useful day out before choosing trees to plant. Buying from a specialist nursery means there will be a knowledgeable salesperson to help with the rootstock and variety choice, but there is a basic guide opposite.

The same variety of apple can make a small or large tree, depending on the type of rootstock on which it is grown.

Buy your chosen varieties on suitable rootstocks. All cultivated apple and pear trees are in fact two trees, the variety grown into the top of a rootstock, which will influence the tree's ultimate size. For growing apples in pots or trained as trees, choose the rootstock M27 or M9. M26 will make a small–medium tree, M111 a larger tree. For pears, a Quince C rootstock will make a smaller tree than Quince A.

Make sure that each tree will have another tree flowering nearby at the same time – each variety will be labelled with its pollination group, so choose trees from the same pollination groups.

Plant

Apples will grow in most soils, and in full sun or dappled shade. Plant bare-root trees in autumn and winter, and pot-grown trees in spring.

Grow

Water young trees as they get established, and trees in pots regularly. Prune apple and pear trees in winter, cutting off any dead or crossing branches to create an open goblet shape for freestanding trees. Never take out over a quarter of the branches in one year.

Trained trees (such as the step-overs below) need additional pruning in summer: cut the side branches back so that each has only three leaves and shorten the main stem to the desired length (e.g. 75cm/30in, for each of the main trained stems for step-overs). In mid-summer, thin the clusters of baby fruits to one or two per group so the rest grow to full size.

Pick

Apples and pears are ready to pick when sweet and their stalk snaps cleanly from the tree when lifted. Pears will need a few days further ripening inside to become soft and juicy.

🌱 PROJECT: Making step-over trees

Young apple and pear trees can be grown into knee-height edging for borders and beds, and still produce a lot of fruit for their size. Look for trees that are specifically bred to be grown as step-over trees and buy when they are one year old ('whips') and have only a single stem.

1. Put in posts of about 65cm (25in), with a wire at 45cm (18in) from the ground.

2. Plant the trees 1.5m (5ft) apart.

3. In spring, carefully bend the tree over and tie it in to the wire, keeping the lower trunk as upright as possible.

4. When the tree sprouts another branch, tie that in going the opposite way along the wire, so each tree covers a total of 1.5m (5ft) in length.

Growing cherries and plums

Cherries and plums each have a short but delicious season, and are perfect straight from the tree.

Varieties to try

• Choose between dessert and cooking plums: 'Early Laxton', 'Victoria' and 'Czar' are all reliable. Why not try a greengage such as 'Cambridge Gage', or a damson tree as well?

• Cherries vary in sweetness, with the acid/sour types such as 'Morello' good to eat but even better for cooking. 'Stella' is a classic sweet variety, or try 'May Duke', which is a cross between a sweet and an acidic cherry.

• Cherry trees on a 'Gisela 5' rootstock are more suitable for small spaces – choose 'Pixy' rootstock for plums in small gardens. Trees labelled as Cinderella or Ballerina have been bred to grow well in pots.

Plant

Give cherries and plums a sunny space. They can be trained in a fan shape against a fence or wall, or grown as freestanding trees. Birds will love the fruit, and trained trees are easiest to protect with netting. Plant bare-root trees in autumn and winter, potted trees in spring.

Grow

Prune in summer, after the fruit is all harvested, aiming to create an open goblet shape for freestanding trees, with no dead or crossing branches. Fan-trained trees need side shoots shortened and branches tied in to create a well-spaced fan shape. Keep trees well-watered, especially when flowering and fruiting.

Pick

Cherries are ready when they are a rich, deep red colour, sweet and juicy. Keep the stalks on the fruit where possible, as they will last longer in the fruit bowl that way.

Plums are ready to pick when they are soft to a gentle squeeze and pull easily from the branch. Watch out for wasps who also love the sweet, juicy fruit!

Bloomin' marvellous

Cherry trees have especially beautiful blossom, produced in spring. Not all cherry trees will produce good fruit – many are ornamental rather than productive. The cherry blossom season in Japan attracts tourists from around the world who come to admire the thousands of flowering trees.

Did you know...

... humans have been eating cherries and plums for thousands of years? The stones and pips/pits of these fruits have been found by archaeologists in prehistoric sites. It is said that to find a Roman road you just need to look for the cherry trees, because the soldiers on the roads spat out the stones as they marched along and these grew new trees.

Growing fruit trees from pips

It takes a long time to grow a fruit tree from seed, but it can be fun, and you get to choose the variety name. This is because all fruit trees you can buy are grown using pieces of other trees, and are therefore clones, but seed-grown trees are all different.

When plants are pollinated it creates a mix of DNA in the seeds between two or more different varieties and, unless carefully controlled by a plant breeder, there is no way of knowing which ones they were. So, trees grown from those seeds will be a completely new variety, unique to your family, and can be given a completely new name.

Citrus fruits come in all shapes and sizes and often cross-pollinate with each other, so for example a seed could grow a cross between a lemon and a kumquat, or a cross between an orange and a lime, and they could have a very unusual shape indeed.

Sowing apple and cherry pips

Clean the pips and sow in a small pot of damp compost – several to one pot is fine. They need to be kept cold (less than 5°C/41°F) for at least two

months – put the pot outside for the winter, or keep it in the fridge (check it remains damp). Then move the pot to a sunny windowsill and keep the compost damp. The pips should sprout in three to eight weeks. Once they are big enough to handle, plant each seedling in its own pot to be grown on.

Sowing citrus pips

Sow clean pips in a pot of damp compost. Put the whole pot in a plastic bag, seal the top and put it somewhere bright and warm (16–21°C/60–70°F inside the bag). Keep the compost damp. Once shoots have appeared (after two to eight weeks), open the bag and grow the seedlings on in a warm, sunny place. When big enough to handle, plant into individual pots and grow on further indoors.

Did you know...

... some citrus seeds display an unusual quirk of nature? They produce more than one shoot/plant from a single seed. This is known as being polyembryonic. Sow the seeds in individual small pots to see more easily if any of them turn out to be polyembryonic – they will need to be separated once big enough to handle. One seedling will grow into the same plant as one of the parent plants, the other will be a cross between the parents.

Get growing... herbs

Herbs, even more so than fruit and vegetables, are much more flavoursome than anything that is available in the shops when they are freshly picked. They are also wonderful for wildlife, especially bees and other pollinating insects, and are pretty, scented plants to have in the garden to boot. Many common garden plants are also classified as herbs – essentially if a plant has a use (be that in the kitchen, in cosmetics or medicine, among other things) it can be called a herb.

This chapter details a few of the most commonly available herbs and some projects to make the most of them, such as home-made pesto, flower crowns and a smelly seat, ideal for a garden reading spot. However, these are just the tip of the iceberg, and there are literally thousands more herbs that can be grown: you might like to choose more plants with which to make fresh herbal drinks, or those that are best for adding to posies of cut flowers, or those that are ideal for using in baking, for example. Use the final section in this chapter to design your own herb garden – small or large – using all your favourite and most useful herbs.

Growing basil

Basil has an incredibly evocative aroma, strongly reminiscent of pizza and pasta, and is best used fresh at the very last minute in cooking to capture its scent.

Varieties to try

- *Ocimum basilicum* is the name for basil, but Greek basil, which has smaller, strongly scented leaves, is called *Ocimum minimum*

- Try 'Genovese' for making pesto, or a purple-leaved variety such as 'Purple Ruffles'.

Sow/Plant

Sow basil seeds in spring. For tender leaves it is best grown inside (in a pot on a sunny windowsill) all summer, as outside the leaves get thicker and tougher.

Alternatively, buy a potted plant of basil from the supermarket. Give it a good water and let it adjust to the new conditions on the windowsill (still in its plastic sleeve) for a few days, then take it out of its pot. Carefully tease the roots/plants into three or four sections and plant each into their own pot (see also p54) to get much bigger, healthier plants for the rest of summer.

Grow

Keep in a warm, sunny spot, rotating regularly so all sides get the best light. Water and feed with a liquid fertiliser regularly.

Pick

Snip or pinch the stems just above a pair of leaves to harvest, then strip the leaves from the stalks. Regular, even picking will keep the plant to size and encourage it to produce more shoots.

GROW

🅥 PROJECT: Make your own pesto

Pesto can be made with any number of herbs (try using parsley, chives, sorrel, wild garlic or carrot leaves), but basil is the traditional Italian version. The nuts used can also be varied – hazelnuts or walnuts work well – so experiment with the family's favourite flavours.

1. Put 100g (3½oz) fresh basil leaves, 25g (1oz) pine nuts, a peeled garlic clove and the zest of half a lemon in a food processor with a glug of olive oil.

2. Blitz until it forms a paste – add more oil if needed.

3. Stir in 50g (1¾oz) of finely grated Parmesan cheese and season to taste.

4. Use straight away by stirring through pasta, or spoon into a clean, sterilised jar, pushing it down to get rid of air bubbles. Pour a layer of olive oil over the top (this will prevent the pesto discolouring) and seal. Keep in the fridge and use within a month, flattening the top and replenishing the oil layer after each use.

Growing thyme and chamomile

Thyme and chamomile are fragrant lower-growing plants, good for an informal edge to the front of borders or planting in pots.

Varieties to try

- Thyme (*Thymus*) has many varieties. It works well with cheese, mushrooms, lamb and many other savoury dishes, but also in sweet dishes. Try lemon or orange thyme for drizzle cakes, or the basic species infused in a chocolate ganache.

- Chamomile (*Chamaemelum*) flowers are used to make a relaxing tea, but the non-flowering 'Treneague' version is better for making fragrant seats and lawns (see opposite).

Plant

Thyme and chamomile both prefer a well-drained soil and a sunny spot, and both will also grow well in pots. Check the label for the variety's specific ultimate height and spread, and give it enough space either side to grow.

Grow

Regular picking will prevent thyme plants becoming straggly; without this, cut them back to half their size after flowering to rejuvenate them. Likewise, chamomile benefits from an annual trim (after flowering) to keep it compact.

Plants can become tired after a few years, with bare stems beneath a few paltry leaves – in this case they are best dug out and replaced.

Pick

Snip off the tops of the stems of thyme, taking evenly from the whole plant. Pick (and dry) chamomile flowers for herbal teas.

GROW

🌱 PROJECT: Make a smelly seat

When sat or trodden on, the plants release their fragrance, so chamomile is ideal for using as a no-mow lawn in areas that don't get a lot of use, or it can be used to make an aromatic occasional garden seat. To use thyme in the same way, choose a creeping variety such as *Thymus serpyllum*.

1. Use a small raised bed, wooden planter or old stone trough (with drainage) to form the seat. Fill with multi-purpose compost and mix in some horticultural grit to aid drainage.

2. Plant the chamomile/thyme in the seat, spacing them 10–15cm (4–6in) apart (so for a seat that measures around 45cm/18in by 30cm/12in, that's 8–12 plants) and water well. Placing them closer will speed up the process of covering the bare soil but does cost more.

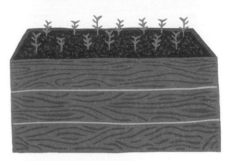

3. Leave for three months before sitting on it, to allow the plants to get established.

4. Trim annually, as shown.

Growing lavender

Beloved of bees as well as people, lavender is a low-maintenance but highly rewarding herb.

Varieties to try

Instantly familiar from its fragrance, there are a few different types of lavender. English lavender (*Lavandula angustifolia*) is the best for cooking: the many varieties include pink- and white-flowered types. French or butterfly lavender (*Lavandula stoechas*) is, while pretty, also toxic and less hardy. *Lavandula* x *intermedia* varieties have a long flowering period.

Plant

Lavender will do best in a well-drained soil in a sunny spot, but it can also be grown in pots. Give plants enough space (refer to the label for its ultimate spread), but for a lavender hedge, plant them closer together by a third or so.

Grow

Once it has finished flowering, cut the soft green/grey stems back hard, but not into the harder brown wood. Older straggly bushes can also be cut back again in spring to form a neat mound, or dig up and replace the plants after 3–5 years.

Pick

Cut the flowers as desired, cutting off a good length of stem and trimming to size afterwards.

🌱 PROJECT: Make a herbal crown or wreath

A floral and fragrant crown is just the thing for summer parties and make-believe play.

1. Twist a piece of sturdy wire into a circle that fits the head of the wearer.

2. Cut stems of lavender, other herbs, sprigs of foliage and/or other flowers, stripping off the lower leaves and leaving around 10cm (4in) of stem below the flowers.

3. Gather the flowers and foliage into small groups and tape them together. Florist's tape is traditionally used, but thin strips of brown kraft or other biodegradable tape means the flowers are more easily composted.

4. Tape the bunches to the wire hoop, so the second bunch overlaps and disguises the stems and tape of the first bunch and so on, until the whole hoop is covered.

5. Spray with water to keep it fresh (store in the fridge if it is to be worn later).

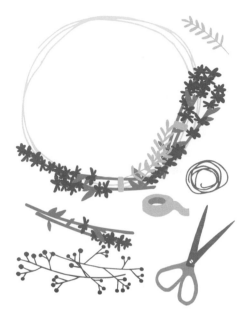

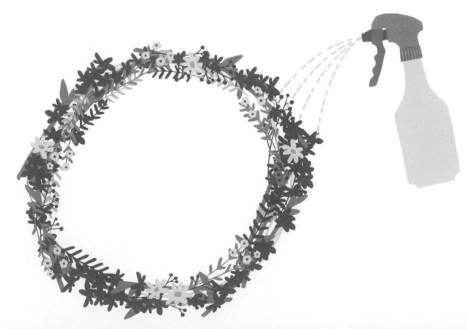

Growing lemon verbena

Brush or rub the leaves of this shrub to release its incredible lemon scent.

Varieties to try

There is only one type of this plant, and its botanical Latin name is *Aloysia citrodora*.

Plant

Lemon verbena can be killed off by a cold, wet winter so either plant it in a very sheltered, sunny place that has well-drained soil, or plant it in a pot that can be moved under cover for the winter. It is deciduous, so its winter shelter doesn't need to be well-lit. Mix some horticultural grit into multi-purpose compost when planting in a pot.

Grown inside all year round, it can keep its leaves through winter as well, but can be more prone to pest infestations.

Grow

Lemon verbena can grow quite large (up to 2.5m/8¼ft tall and wide), but when cut regularly to use in the kitchen or flower arrangements it can be easily kept to a smaller size. In spring, cut back any longer stems to make a strong, open framework of lower branches.

Pick

Cut stems, then pick off the leaves to use in the kitchen.

🌱 PROJECT: Make a box of tea

Lemon verbena is a great plant to use for fresh herbal teas. Why not plant up a few pots of herbs good for tea? Presented together in a basket or crate, they would make a lovely gift.

Collect small plants of lemon verbena, peppermint, lemon balm and fennel. Plant into pretty pots (why not paint them, or tie ribbons around them?) and make a label for each one. Group together into a container to give away, or put them outside the back door where they will always be in reach for a cup of fresh herbal tea.

1. To make tea with fresh herbs, pick a couple of sprigs of the herb (try combining them to make, for example, mint and lemon balm or fennel and mint) and rinse in cold water to get rid of any dust or bugs.

2. Put the herbs in the bottom of a mug with a splash of cold water. Boil the kettle, then wait for a couple of minutes before pouring over the herbs.

3. Steep and remove the herbs, or leave them in for a stronger taste while drinking.

Growing mint and lemon balm

Mint and lemon balm can be grown in the same way.

Varieties to try

Lemon balm (*Melissa officinalis*) is the only one of its type, but there is also a 'Lime Balm' variety.

Mint comes in many different varieties: black peppermint, 'Moroccan' and 'Berber' mint are best for teas and drinks; spearmint for mint sauce; then there are many different flavoured mints from chocolate to strawberry – be sure to crush and smell a leaf before buying to make sure it is what it says on the label.

Plant

Mint is notorious for spreading everywhere, but this can be easily prevented. Either plant in a large pot, from whence it cannot spread, or plant in a large pot that is then plunged into open ground. Keep the lip of the pot slightly above soil level and just trim off the low-growing, spreading stems (stolons) as they creep over the edge of the pot.

Both mint and lemon balm will tolerate partial or dappled shade and prefer damp, rich soil.

Grow

The stems of both plants will die back in autumn – leave the dead stems to shelter wildlife for winter and cut back in early spring before the new shoots begin to grow.

Trim the spreading stolons of mint as required.

Pick

Cut the stems when needed.

🍃 PROJECT: Make new plants from cut stems in water

Mint will make new roots when a cut stem is placed in water, so it is easy to create new plants to give away or plant elsewhere in the garden. The new plants can also be grown indoors on a sunny windowsill, where they should stay green through winter, giving fresh herbs when the outdoor plants have died back.

1. Cut a few healthy, green stems of mint (preferably with no flowers on them), about 20cm (8in) long, and strip off the lower leaves.

2. Put into a glass of water and leave on a sunny windowsill. Change the water every couple of days.

3. After a while, the stems will produce roots on their lower half. Once these have grown to a few centimetres long, take them out of the glass and plant each one into its own small pot, being careful not to damage the roots.

4. Water well and grow on in the pot until the roots have filled it, then plant into a bigger pot.

Mint makes a great herbal tea, and can also be used for home-made mint sauce or jelly or for mint-choc chip ice cream. It pairs really well with melon and watermelon in a fruit salad, and try adding fresh leaves to other salads and vegetable dishes too – it goes particularly well with peas, beans and courgettes.

Growing edible flowers

Edible flowers are often planted alongside herbs (indeed, many herb flowers are also edible), and make pretty additions to cakes, bakes and salads.

Varieties to try

Cakes and other bakes are best decorated with sweet flowers, such as:

- Violas
- Primroses
- Sweet violet
- Roses
- Lavender
- Scented pelargoniums
- Thyme
- Lemon verbena.

Many other edible flowers have a peppery or savoury taste, such as:

- Nasturtiums
- Rocket
- Borage.

Finally, the flowers of herbs usually used for their leaves can also be eaten, such as:

- Basil
- Rosemary
- Wild garlic
- Chives
- Oregano
- Fennel (try the pollen as a garnish).

Plant/Sow

Edible flowers are best grown in pots or raised beds, where they are less likely to get splashed with mud or otherwise get dirty (they cannot be washed before using). Try a pot of spring primroses and violas planted under some lemon verbena, or grow scented pelargoniums as houseplants.

Nasturtiums are a super plant to grow with other vegetables – climbing varieties will scramble up a wigwam, while others will trail from a hanging basket or over the edge of a raised bed. Sow seeds in early spring (either direct or in pots to then plant out).

Sow borage seeds in spring, either direct or in small pots that are then planted out.

Grow

Primroses and violas need little attention. Nasturtiums can be prone to blackfly – pinch out the affected parts as soon as they are seen. Borage can need the support of other plants around it or tie it loosely to a pole.

Pick

Pick the flowers immediately before they are needed, or store in a tin or box in the fridge. Remove the green stem and small leaves (sepals) at the base of the flower, and check for insects.

🌱 PROJECT: Make flower ice cubes

Borage and violas in particular are good candidates for freezing into ice cubes for summer drinks or toddler sensory play.

1. Half-fill an ice cube tray with water.

2. Add one flower to each compartment, pushing it in carefully so it is flat and slightly submerged, if possible.

3. Put in the freezer for four to five hours, then take out the tray, top it up with more water and return it to the freezer.

Design a herb garden

A herb garden can take up as much or as little space as there is to spare, and is a great opportunity to be creative in the garden. Traditionally, herb gardens were laid out in formal, geometric patterns, such as in the gardens of Tudor kings and queens, but so long as all the plants have enough space and the right soil and light to grow well, they can be arranged in whatever pattern suits your space and family best.

Find the space

First, choose a space for the herb garden, preferably in full sun. Measure the area so it can be planned on a piece of paper.

Choose the plants

Decide what kind of plants are going in the garden – think about their relative heights, colours, shapes and textures, as well as which ones are most useful and pretty.

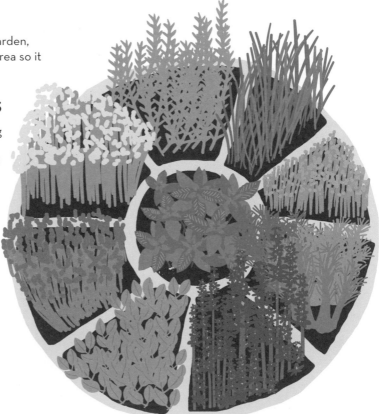

CIRCULAR designs work well with a central focal point, such as a clipped bay tree or fennel plant.

Design the layout, and plant

Do this on a piece of paper first, to see how the chosen plants will best combine into an attractive, useful and coherent garden. Use different colours for each type of plant and use a scale ruler, if possible, to more easily calculate the numbers needed for each plant. Then lay out the plants on the prepared ground (see p14–17) and move them as needed, not planting until the layout is final.

*SQUARE or **RECTANGULAR** beds easily compartmentalise the different herbs. Add paths if necessary to avoid compacting the soil while picking.*

INFORMAL herb patches allow for more aesthetic flow between the different herb plants, but can still be productive and useful. Plant in groups of three, five or seven plants for each herb type in larger beds.

Get growing...
flowers and
wildlife gardens

Although gardens can provide harvests of fruit, vegetables and herbs, they can also be enjoyed just for themselves. Grow plants simply for the joy of growing them, for nurturing them from a seed all the way to flowering. Grow flowers for a riot of colour or for a calming pastel or white haven away from the hustle and bustle of the busy streets. Flowers and leaves are full of fascinating detail – ideal for sketching, painting or printing with – and also provide homes for a huge variety of wildlife.

This chapter shows how to grow different types of plants to fill the garden, what to grow for a few posies of home-grown cut flowers, and some ideas of how best to garden with wildlife in mind. Finally, why not create a living sculpture out of willow or a tiny pond?

Types of flowers

Plants come in all manner of shapes and sizes, so there is something suitable for all gardeners and gardens. Some grow quickly, some slowly; some grow big and some very small. Remember to choose the right plant for the place and you can't go wrong.

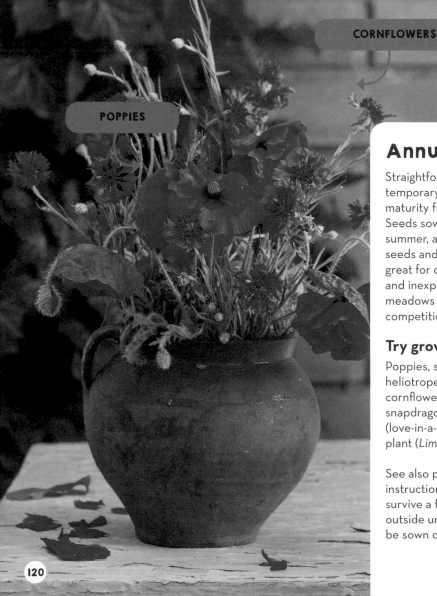

CORNFLOWERS

POPPIES

Annual plants

Straightforward, rewarding and temporary, annual plants are grown to maturity from seed in a single year. Seeds sown in spring will flower in summer, and then the plants make new seeds and die in autumn. Annuals are great for creating a relatively instant and inexpensive garden; for wildflower meadows and for sunflower-growing competitions.

Try growing...

Poppies, sunflowers, marigolds, heliotrope (it smells like cherry pie), cornflowers, sweet peas, cosmos, snapdragons, cleome, zinnia, nigella (love-in-a-mist) and the poached egg plant (*Limnanthes*).

See also p52 and check the seed packet instructions – some flowers will not survive a frost and cannot be put outside until early summer, others can be sown direct outside.

Herbaceous perennials

These plants are temporary above ground and permanent below it. Their roots survive for many years, producing new shoots every spring that grow and flower through summer, but that then die back in autumn and are cut off to make way for the following year's new stems. They can be sown from seed but for a bigger plant instantly, they can be bought in pots once already a year or two old.

Try growing...

Geraniums, rudbeckia, echinacea, sedums, salvia (e.g. 'Caradonna'), geums, lady's mantle (*Alchemilla mollis*), lamb's ears (*Stachys byzantina*), erigeron/Mexican fleabane, chocolate cosmos, fennel, mint and lemon balm.

ECHINACEA

Shrubs

Shrubs or bushes have woody stems that stay on the plant all year, and leaves that can be evergreen or deciduous. They can be large or small, and add structure to a garden. Most will need pruning (cutting back) to some degree – a good rule of thumb is to do this after flowering, but check the specific requirements using the RHS website or pruning books.

Try growing...

Lavender and other herbs, currants and other fruits, smoke bush (*Cotinus*), pittosporum, daphne, roses and Japanese acers.

ROSEMARY

MINT

CHIVES

ROSE

Climbers

Climbing plants can turn a drab wall or a suntrap into a lush, relaxing haven. They have long stems that either stick to the walls themselves, will twine themselves onto wires, trellis or other supports, or require tying in to supports. They can also be trained over pergolas and archways, and annual climbers can be grown up wigwams or poles. Check their pruning requirements with the RHS website or books.

Try growing...

Climbing roses, wisteria, honeysuckle, Virginia creeper, Boston ivy, clematis and jasmine.

Climbing annuals: cup-and-saucer plant, ipomoea, black-eyed Susan (*Thunbergia*).

A cut flower patch

Many cut flowers available to buy in the shops are flown hundreds of miles to get here. Seasonal flowers picked from the garden have zero air miles and a more personal touch.

A cut flower patch can be as large or small as you have space for, but even a small area can produce a lot of blooms. Cut flowers can be annuals, bulbs, herbaceous perennials or shrubs. The design is a chance to get creative; just make sure there is space between the plants to access for picking, and that the roots of permanent plants don't get disturbed by planting and removing annuals. Because the plants will be continually cut back as the blooms are picked, it's possible to plant them slightly closer together than the usual spacing (usually found on the label, or refer to the RHS website).

When cutting flowers to put in a vase, cut as long a stem as needed, making the cut just above where a leaf is growing from the stem. The plant can then sprout new shoots from that point with no ugly stub of stem dying back above it.

ALLIUM

DAFFODIL

COSMOS

LILY

CORNFLOWER

Pick of the bunch

Good annual cut flowers

Cornflowers, sweet peas, marigolds, sunflowers, snapdragons, cosmos, ammi, gypsophila, dahlias, dill.

Good bulbs for cut flowers

Daffodils, tulips, gladioli, lilies, alliums, dahlias (technically a tuber, and not frost hardy).

Good perennials and shrubs for cut flowers

Lavender, roses, ornamental grasses, *Alchemilla mollis* (lady's mantle), ornamental cherry trees, honeysuckle, forsythia, hydrangeas, astrantia.

Good perennials and shrubs for foliage

Mint, lemon balm, eucalyptus, bay/laurel, pittosporum and purple cotinus. Fern foliage is good for a different texture.

A pot of flowers for every season

With just two or three pots it's possible to have something looking good for each season. Rotate the pots to ring in the changes.

Spring pot

In autumn, plant a pot with a 'bulb lasagne'. This layering method of planting with different bulbs allows for a single pot to house flowers over a long period. The bulbs should be spaced around 4–5cm (1³/4–2in) apart in each layer, for up to three layers.

Fill the base of the pot with 10cm (4in) of multipurpose compost. Arrange the bottom layer of bulbs on top, pointy end up. These should be the latest flowering, largest bulbs (e.g. tulips). Cover with a layer of compost and repeat once or twice more with smaller and smaller bulbs (e.g. daffodils in the middle, then snowdrops, iris or muscari on top), finishing with layer of compost. Water well, and leave until spring, watering in dry spells.

Summer pot

Annual bedding plants are easy to come by in spring. Choose some trailing (e.g. lobelia or petunia), some bushy (e.g. busy lizzies or rudbeckia) and one or two tall plants (e.g. cosmos or nicotiana) to create a full pot. It will need regular watering and feeding, and protection from frost, but will flower freely all summer long.

Autumn pot

Ornamental grasses are really attractive in autumn,
when they collect beads of dew or jagged frost
along their blades. Choose a single plant or a few
(plants always look better in groups of odd
numbers) to plant. The grasses are perennial, so
look after the pot for the rest of the year, ready to
bring it back again into the display spot next
autumn. Try *Pennisetum* 'Red Bunny Tails' for its
fluffy seedheads.

Winter pot

Make a wintery forest by planting a pot with dwarf
conifer trees. These come in different shades of
green and grey, and different forms. They can even
be festooned for the holidays with miniature lights
and decorations. These trees will only grow slowly,
so with good care can be kept in the pot and
rotated through many more seasons to come.

Where the wild things are

A garden full of minibeasts and other wildlife is not only good for the environment and for helping the garden itself thrive, but is also fascinating for budding naturalists. See also p130 for how to create a mini pond to attract water insects and amphibians. Make the garden wildlife-friendly by incorporating a few of these suggestions:

A garden for minibeasts

Leave some of the garden untidy – allow autumn leaves to pile up in a corner, let nettles (a valuable food source for butterflies and their caterpillars) grow in a contained, out-of-the-way area.

Leave stems of herbaceous perennials standing through winter instead of cutting them down in autumn – their hollow stems are ideal hiding places.

Plant nectar-rich plants for bees and butterflies – look out for the RHS 'Perfect for Pollinators' bee symbol on plant labels.

Dead wood is dead good – old stumps and log piles are heaven for minibeasts if there is space to leave some undisturbed.

A garden for birds

Hang up bird feeders of seed and fatty treats – squidge some peanut butter into pine cones and hang them up or hang up an apple for home-made feeders. Keep them topped up year round so the birds can rely on them.

Plant trees with fruit and berries for the birds, such as hawthorn, wild cherry and crab apple.

Put up nesting boxes.

Provide a water bath in which the birds can drink and wash.

◑ PROJECT: Grow your own birdseed

When sunflowers have finished flowering, cut down the stalk but don't throw the flowerhead on the compost. Tie some string securely around it and hang it upside down – the birds will love to peck out the seeds.

Leave the seedheads of other plants standing over winter too, such as fennel, ornamental grasses, teasels and ornamental thistles. Wildlife can use them for food and shelter during autumn and winter. They also look great in dried flower arrangements.

A pond in a bucket

Make a miniature pond and watch the insect and bird life flock to it. It may even get a resident frog or toad.

What to use

Any watertight container can be used for a pond. Wooden half barrels need to be filled with water and continually topped up until the wood has swelled enough that it stops leaking.

If the pond is big enough for birds, frogs, toads or small mammals to get into, they need to have a means of getting out, as they cannot climb smooth upright sides. Securely wedge a piece of wood into the container to make a ramp or step. Cover it tightly with chicken wire to make it less slippery.

Preparing the pond

Fill the pond with water from a water butt or tap (leave tap water for a few days before planting).

Make shelves for the marginal plants' pots to sit on around the edge of the pond. Check the requirements of the plants (it should be on the label): some will need to have their pot 5cm (2in) under the water, others up to 15cm (6in). Stand the pots on bricks (or similar) at the right depth.

Plants to use

Choose at least one each of marginal, floating and oxygenating plants – more if the pond is larger and has the space. All these plants are suited to small and mini ponds, but browse the selection at garden centres, online and at aquatic centres.

Marginal plants

- Sweet flag (*Acorus gramineus* var. *pusillus*) – a grass up to 12cm (4¾in) tall
- Brooklime (*Veronica beccabunga*) has blue and white flowers
- Water iris (*Iris laevigata*)
- Corkscrew rush (*Juncus effusus* f. *spiralis*)
- Water forget-me-not (*Myosotis scorpioides*).

Floating plants

- Water lily (*Nymphaea odorata* var. *minor* or any *Nymphaea* 'Pygmaea' variety)
- Frogbit (*Hydrocharis morsus-ranae*).

Oxygenating plants

- Water violet (*Hottonia palustris*)
- Hair grass (*Eleocharis acicularis*).

RAMP FOR WILDLIFE
It's ideal to have one they can use to both enter and exit.

Art in the garden

A garden, no matter what size or form it takes, can be an endless source of inspiration to the artist. There is always something new to see and draw, paint, write about or sculpt, but the garden can also be used to create art in itself.

🌱 PROJECT: Living sculpture

Willow trees are very easy to grow, and their long, flexible stems make them ideal for weaving into a living sculpture or play area. Growing willow in this way is actually growing from hardwood cuttings – a technical name for taking a piece of woody stem and sticking it in the ground! Willow grows best in a damp soil, and will tolerate dappled shade.

Decide what kind of sculpture to make – perhaps a simple domed den, tunnel or fairy house, or a more elaborate ship, or an abstract shape of flowing lines that suit the willow's bendy form – then create a living sculpture following the steps below:

1. Take a number of pieces of willow stem (they will need to be spaced 10–20cm/4–8in, apart, depending on the design), cut from a healthy tree or two in early spring before the leaves come out, or buy a bundle of stems locally or online.

2. Cut one end of each stem pointed so they all go in the ground the right way up.

3. Make holes in the soil in the right places for the sculpture with a bamboo pole or screwdriver, then push in the willow deeply and wait until spring, when they should sprout leaves and branches. To make a more solid-looking sculpture, put some pieces in at a 45° angle to create crossing stems. These can be tied to the uprights to start with until they have grown into place.

4. As the stems grow taller, weave them together to create the sculpture. It may take only one year to finish, or more ambitious, larger projects may need several years of growth to complete the design.

5. Once it is the right shape, wayward and extra stems can be trimmed off or tied in every summer.

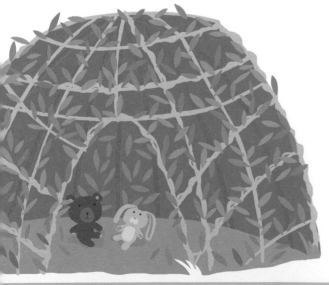

◐ PROJECT: Decorate clay pots and coasters

Use garden plants to create pretty botanical coasters and pots from air-drying clay.

1. Collect interesting pieces from the garden such as seedheads (e.g. poppies, irises and grasses), flowers, leaves and twigs.

2. Roll, cut and/or sculpt the clay into the desired shapes, then press the garden pieces into it to make an impression of the outline and as much detail as possible.

3. Allow the clay to dry completely before painting, either washing in a single colour and/or picking out individual details.

Get growing... houseplants

Although social media can give the impression that houseplants have only been around for the last few years, the desire to be surrounded by greenery is as old as mankind itself. Houseplants can bring life to a room, introduce fresh ingredients to a kitchen windowsill and inspire curiosity about the weird and wonderful world of plants. They can make us more relaxed and also make our air cleaner by filtering out the pollutants and toxins.

Houseplants can be part of the décor, or they can be part of the family, passed down the generations and nurtured as we would a pet. There is a houseplant for every part of the house – be it sunny or shady, hot or cold – so why not try growing one or two?

Desert landscape - growing succulents

When it comes to getting growing indoors, there are few groups of plants as cool or as easy to grow as succulents. They are mostly desert plants, adapted to grow with minimal water and in dry air, just like our centrally heated homes. They are also quite easy to get hold of (at pocket-money prices for the smallest pots) from most garden centres and other plant shops – look out for them in supermarkets, too.

Spot the succulent

Some have spikes to fend off animals that might try to eat them for their sweet, sappy leaves.

Fleshy leaves or adapted leaves for water storage.

Funky shapes and patterns formed by the foliage.

Slow growing.

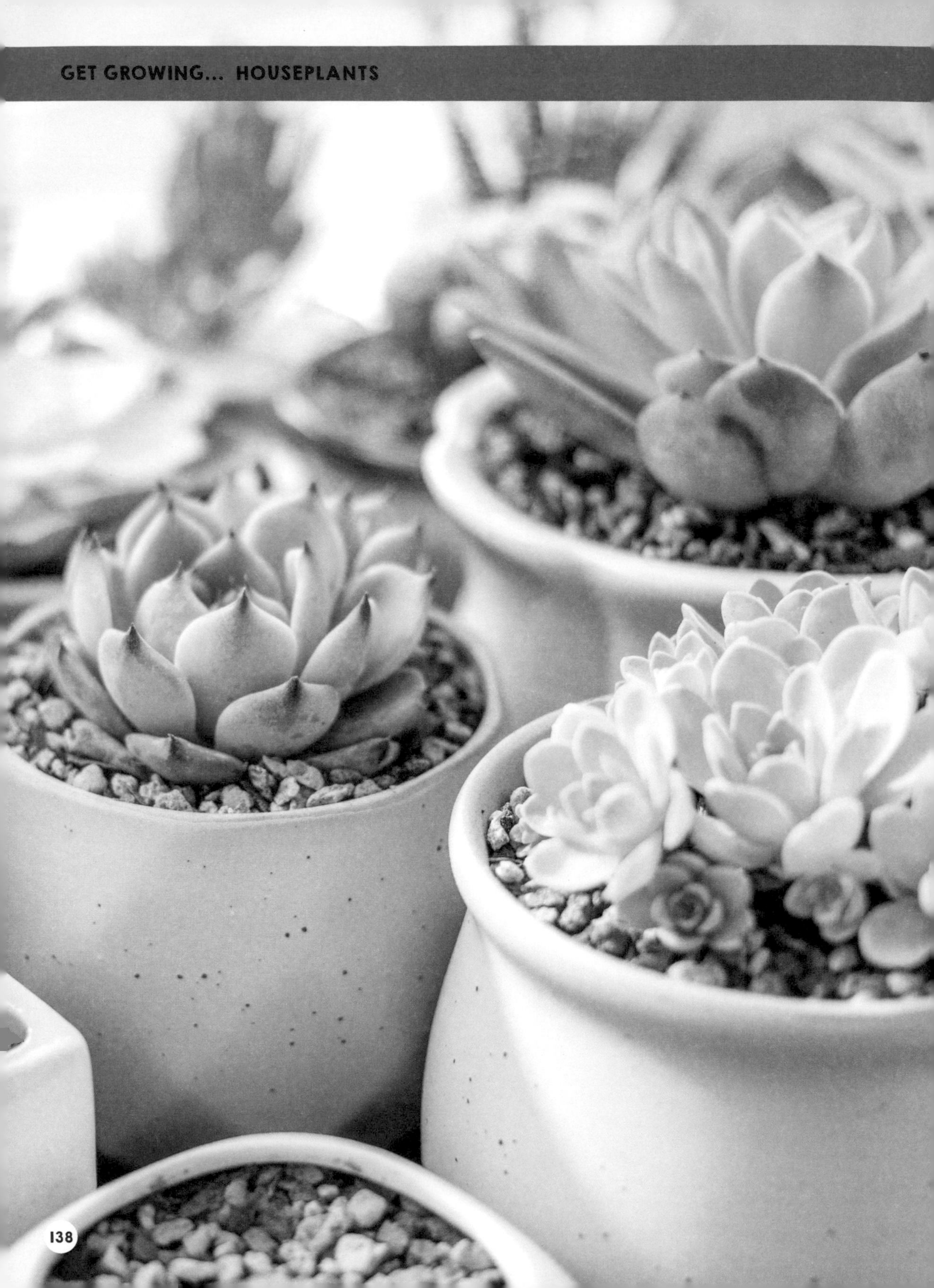

Growing succulents and cacti

Try to mimic their origins as far as possible – giving desert plants the sunniest, warmest spots in the house. However, *Epiphyllum* and *Schlumbergera* come from rainforests, so check the label.

Water when the soil is almost completely dry, and make sure they are never sitting in wet soil or a pool of water at the bottom of the pot.

Give them a dilute liquid fertiliser through spring and summer.

Re-pot annually to refresh the compost and/or increase the pot size if they are getting pot bound. Use a free-draining mix of compost and grit or a proprietary cacti compost.

Thick gardening gloves are best for handling cacti, and a pair of tweezers is useful for picking out old flowers and debris from among the spikes.

Legend has it...

... that when a money tree (*Crassula ovata*) flowers, its owner will come into a fortune.

Did you know...

... all cacti are succulents, but not all succulents are cacti? Only cacti have areoles from which spines can grow; the spikes on succulents are part of the leaves, like on a holly tree.

⊘ PROJECT: Take a shelfie

- Use the different forms and colours of the succulents to make a patterned planter...

- ... or pot them individually and display as a collection. A unifying style or colour of pot helps complete the look.

- Pretend the spiky forms are different punk hairdos: stick on some googly eyes or paint a face on the pot beneath.

Good plants to try

Succulents
- *Aeonium arboreum* 'Atropurpureum'
- *Agave americana*
- *Agave parryi*
- *Aloe vera*
- *Crassula*
- *Echeveria*
- *Lithops karasmontana*
- *Rhipsalis*
- *Senecio.*

Cacti
- *Mammillaria bombycina*
- *Ferocactus glaucescens*
- *Opuntia.*

Leafy plants

Not all houseplants need to be on a sunny windowsill; many just need a bright spot out of direct sunlight. For plants more suited to shadier rooms, see pp150–151.

Palms

Most of the houseplants for sale in garden and home stores are palms, with glossy green leaves often held on long stalks. Technically, a palm is one whose leaves are divided into individual leaflets – often in the shape of a hand: the 'palm'.

The dwarf mountain palm (*Chamaedorea elegans*) can usually be found to purchase in various sizes. It needs little maintenance other than watering and feeding, an annual re-pot and the removal of dead leaves.

For a houseplant that looks like a miniature version of the palm trees found on the streets of Los Angeles, try the dwarf fan palm, *Chamaerops humilis*. It can also be moved outside in summer. Look after it as for the mountain palm (above).

To fill an empty corner, try the flat palm (*Howea forsteriana*), which adds a jungly feel to any room.

Others to try

Although it is unlikely the plant will ever actually grow any beans, the coffee plant makes a good houseplant. It's also often available as a kit to start from seed. Care for it as for the mountain palm (above), and additionally pinch out the tips of young plants to encourage bushy growth.

In a very warm and humid room, such as a consistently warm bathroom, why not try growing a chocolate plant? They have even been known to produce pods of cocoa beans in UK glasshouses.

Clivia have long, strappy leaves and exotic bright orange or red flowers. They are fairly robust, and need a colder spell to produce the flowers, so a conservatory is the ideal place for them.

PALM

CLIVIA

The mists of time

The air in most homes tends to be dry, especially in rooms heated by radiators. Leafy houseplants need a bit more humidity, so remembering to mist them all every day will help keep them healthy and green. Simply fill a spray bottle with water and squirt a gentle mist all over the plant – an ideal job for young gardeners.

Plants for free - pups and cuttings

Some houseplants multiply themselves relatively easily, and the gardener can take advantage of this to quickly increase their number of plants. Once established, the new plants can be kept, given away or perhaps sold (a good way for children to learn about the basics of business).

Pups

This is the name given to the mini-me versions of themselves that succulents produce. They can be spotted on older plants, usually growing around the base of the plant.

Use a sharp knife to sever the pup(s) from the main plant, trying to keep a small piece of root attached as well, if possible. Pot the pup(s) into small pots of a compost/grit mix.

Leaf cuttings

Other plants have a cunning trick of growing new plantlets from a single leaf, which makes for a fun and fascinating way to multiply stocks of plants. Cuttings are best taken in spring and early summer.

Plants that can be propagated by leaf cuttings include African violet (*Streptocarpus*, also known as *Saintpaulia*), *Begonia*, *Sansevieria trifasciata* (mother-in-law's tongue), *Kalanchoe*, *Echeveria*, *Crassula ovata* (the jade tree) and indoor sedums.

For succulent plants

Cut or gently crack a few healthy leaves away from the stem. Leave in a dry, sunny place for one or two days so that the wounded part calluses over, then insert into a pot of compost/grit mix.

For streptocarpus and begonia

Take a healthy leaf and slice it along the midrib (the central 'vein' running along the length of the leaf). Make a shallow trench in a tray of compost/grit mix and insert the half leaf, cut side down. Pin it down over the midrib by piercing the leaf with a half paperclip and hooking it over. Alternatively, for *Streptocarpus*, simply pin down a whole leaf flat onto the surface of the compost.

For mother-in-law's tongue

Slice a healthy leaf into crossways sections and push each into a pot of compost/grit mix so that they stand up.

Aftercare

Keep the surface of the compost just moist, not wet, and mist the pots daily. Small plantlets should start to grow along the cut edges or midribs of the leaves, pups will form their own roots. Once big enough to handle, gently separate the new plants and their roots from the leaf and plant into their own small pots to grow on.

MOTHER-IN-LAW'S TONGUE

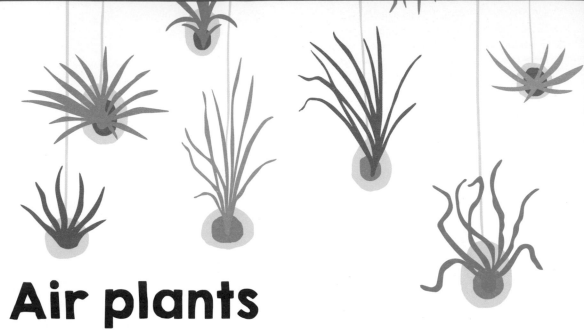

Air plants

Surely some of the coolest houseplants around are those that need no soil or pot at all. Air plants are generally green-blue-grey in appearance, and can either be stringy or rosette-shaped. They have no obvious roots or stems, and have evolved to absorb not only water but also nutrients from the air through tiny pores in their foliage.

How to care for them

Air plants are low-maintenance houseplants, but not no-maintenance. As most houses are not as humid as the rainforests they like to grow in, they will need additional watering by plunging them into tepid water two to three times a week. Rainwater (or soft tap water) is best if possible. Dry rosette plants upside down so water doesn't collect in the leaves and encourage rotting.

Alternatively, keep in a more humid (bath)room and give an additional misting every other day.

Add orchid fertiliser to the water of the spray bottle or plunging bowl once a month (leave the plant in water for two hours on these occasions).

Cut out any dead leaves or flowers as required.

How to display them

Air plants sometimes come mounted on pieces of driftwood or shells, or you can create a more personal display. Glass bowls that are open on one side can be hung from the ceiling and the air plant housed inside, or they could be put onto another houseplant.

Suspend a single specimen or a collection into an empty picture frame, balance them on vases, or hang them using invisible thread or fishing line so it looks like they are floating – the possibilities are wide and varied when a plant needs no soil!

Ensure they are placed in bright light, but not direct sunlight.

How do they grow in the wild?

Air plants belong to a group of plants called epiphytes. In the wild they would grow attached to the branches or trunks of trees, rocks or anywhere they can make space for themselves, much as moss and lichen grow on trees and rooftops. They use the host structure for support, but don't feed off it. (Mistletoe grows on trees, but also takes nutrients from them, so it is a parasite not an epiphyte.)

Buyer beware!

It is always a good idea to make sure plants have come from a reputable source when choosing them at the garden centre, but air plants especially are sometimes harvested unsustainably from the wild. Make sure the vendor of your air plants can account for their home-grown or sustainable origin.

Grow a living screen

It is much easier to grow trailing plants indoors than out, as there are many more possibilities of where to house their pots – on bookshelves, on top of kitchen cabinets or shelves, wall-mounted or above stairs and hanging down from the ceiling. Trailing houseplants can be hung more or less anywhere and can help to create a real jungle feel, as well as more restful green tones.

Some climbers will also happily trail downwards or can be trained (tied to a support or framework to encourage the stems to grow a certain way) to create a living screen of plants over a doorway or archway, or to divide a room.

Watering hanging plants

To avoid drips, trailing plants are generally planted into a lightweight pot that is then housed within a more attractive outer planter that is either hung up or placed on a high surface.

To water them, check the moisture level in the compost with a finger first, then water slowly, allowing each addition to be soaked up before adding the next and avoiding excess water pooling in the base of the outer planter. If possible, take the whole thing down to water it.

Pruning trailing and climbing plants

To avoid climbing or trailing plants taking over the room entirely, some pruning will be necessary. Simply snip off the ends of the stems when they get too long, always making a neat cut just above a bud or leaf. Wayward stems of climbers can be trained in or pruned off as necessary.

Good trailing plants to grow

- Chain of hearts (*Ceropegia woodii*)

- *Epipremnum*

- *Hoya carnosa*

- *Hoya linearis*

- *Hoya gracilis*

- Ivy (*Hedera* spp)

- *Peperomia prostrata*

- *Sedum morganianum*

- String of pearls (*Senecio rowleyanus*).

Good climbing houseplants to grow

All climb but need supports and tying in to a framework or trellis.
- Jasmine

- Passion flower (*Passiflora* spp)

- Swiss Cheese plant (*Monstera deliciosa*).

Has something been eating my cheese plant?

The Swiss Cheese plant is so-called because its leaves are full of holes, just like some cheeses (although the botanical Latin name is also pretty cool: *Monstera deliciosa*). Usually, holes in a plant's leaves indicate that something has been eating it, and it's bad news, but this plant just grows that way. They are native to jungle understoreys, where bright light is rare. Their dark green leaves absorb what they can in the shade, but when a beam of direct sunlight hits their leaves, they actually don't want to absorb all of it as it would result in an unsustainable growth spurt. The holes let some of the light through and the *Monstera* can continue its slow, steady climb up the trunk on which it is growing.

Carnivorous plants

There is always an exception to the rule, and carnivorous plants are definitely exceptional in the world of plants. Gruesome and fascinating, they evolved in bogs, swamps and other places where nutrients (especially nitrogen) in the soil are hard to access, so instead they supplement their diet by trapping flies and other insects in their flowers and 'eating' them.

The Venus fly trap is probably the most well-known carnivorous plant, but there are other types as well. Some snap shut on their insect victims, like the Venus fly trap, and slowly digest them; others grow long tubes known as pitchers – the insect enters the top of the pitcher, falls in and at the bottom is digested in a pool of acid.

Carnivorous plants take a little more care than the average houseplant, and different conditions to most – they need to be in constant water, for example, in order to mimic their swampy origins. The plants below are the most common, but visiting a specialist nursery can be a good way to really get to grips with these grisly bug-eaters.

Venus fly trap (*Dionaea muscipula*)

A colourful and fun little plant, it will need bright (not direct) light and humid conditions, a saucer full of rainwater for the pot to sit in and a ready supply of flies. Never cause the traps to shut without anything inside as this will not benefit the plant.

Pitcher plants (*Sarracenia*)

Some are hardy enough to grow outside in a large pot of peaty compost, others will need the protection of a greenhouse or conservatory in winter. They need a bright, sunny windowsill. Keep the pot standing in a pool of rainwater. If they don't seem to be catching enough flies inside through summer, move them outside.

Monkey cups (*Nepenthes*)

The cups of these plants are actually the leaves, evolved by the plant to catch bugs, and the flowers are small and insignificant. These types do not need to stand in water, but do need very high humidity – the two main groups come from highland forests or lowland swamps – and high daytime and night-time temperatures. They could therefore be grown in a hanging basket in a bathroom or greenhouse.

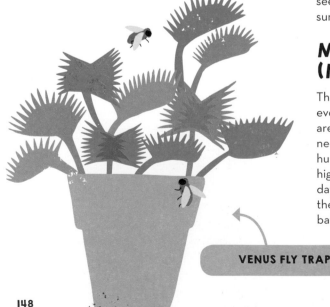

VENUS FLY TRAP

MONKEY CUPS

149

Jungle plants and ferns

If a plant naturally grows in shaded places, such as woodlands and jungles, it will grow perfectly well in a shaded part of a house. Ferns like damp, shaded places, so with a bit of misting can make great houseplants. Good choices include the cast iron plant (*Aspidistra elatior*), the bird's nest fern (*Asplenium nidus*) and the Delta maidenhair fern (*Adiantum raddianum*).

Spider plants (*Chlorophytum comosum*) are not ferns, but will also happily grow in a shadier spot in the house. They are excellent at filtering and purifying air. Long, strappy leaves (the commonly found variegated version has a white stripe down each leaf) grow up then cascade over the edge of the pot like hair. Stems ('runners') with flowers and mini-plantlets hang down – pot up the plantlets for new plants (see below). Hang it or put it on a high shelf, it reaches about 50cm (20in) tall and wide.

Runners: free plants

Some plants multiply themselves by producing new small plants (plantlets) on a long stem, or runner, that grows out of the plant. In a garden setting, these runners would continue to grow along the ground and the plantlets would root wherever they could find space. Strawberries and spider plants are known for this trait, and in the garden, creeping buttercup is considered a weed because of it.

To take advantage of these free plants, simply provide them with a point at which to root. For strawberries growing in the ground, this could be just pushing the plantlet into the soil. For spider plants or pot-grown strawberries (or when the new plants are to be given away), put a few pots, filled with compost, around the base of the mother plant. Use small wire hoops (e.g. half a paperclip) to pin down the plantlet onto the compost surface.

Cut off the rest of the runner beyond the plantlet, but leave the plantlets connected to the mother plant until they have rooted into the pot. Once the plantlets are growing by themselves, cut the runner stem from the mother plant and the plantlet.

Do this with only the first plantlet on each runner, but each mother plant will provide at least three new plants every year.

What to do with your garden in...

Your garden can be a source of entertainment, relaxation, learning and inspiration all year round. It also needs some attention throughout the year, whether it be weeding or watering. Looking after a garden is half the fun of having one, and 20 minutes' care here and there can be all it needs to thrive.

Getting out into the garden every day is a great way to appreciate the changing seasons – to watch flowers come and go, leaves flourish in spring and fall in autumn, the sparkle of morning dew on the grass or frost on bare branches, these are all reminders of the wonders of plants and nature. The following notes are a guide to the main tasks for each season and ideas for garden activities and projects. For more detailed information on the seasonal care of particular plants, see the RHS website.

... Spring

Fruit, veg and herbs

- Prepare beds and pots for sowing.

- Sow seeds direct or in pots to plant out in early summer.

- Pull out baby weeds as they emerge.

- Cut back straggly lavender plants to a compact framework.

- Repot or add a layer of fresh compost to the tops of permanent pot plantings.

- Plant bare-root or potted fruit trees and bushes.

- Protect fruit blossoms from frost, where possible, with horticultural fleece or similar.

- Protect emerging potato shoots from the frost with a layer of horticultural fleece or several sheets of newspaper, if necessary.

- Water plants as needed, taking care especially of potted plants.

Flowers

- Protect young plants from slugs and snails with regular patrols or traps.

- Prune roses.

- Repot or add a layer of fresh compost to the tops of permanent pot plantings.

- Herbaceous perennials that have grown too large can be divided: split the rootball of the plant with a sharp spade into two, three or four sections, removing all but one and backfilling the hole. The split-off sections can be planted elsewhere or potted up to give away.

- Sow seeds direct or in pots to plant out in early summer.

- Plant bulbs of summer flowers (e.g. gladioli, lilies).

- Tie in new growth of climbing plants.

- Put in supports for tall plants and climbers before they need it.

- Re-pot and start feeding houseplants.

- Water plants as needed, taking care especially of potted plants.

Trees and shrubs

· Plant bare-root or potted trees and shrubs.

· Cut back the stems of willow (Salix) and dogwood (Cornus).

Lawns

· Rake (scarify) in early spring to remove old grass, leaves and moss.

· Make air holes with a garden fork (aerate) to relieve compaction and waterlogging.

· Scatter grass seed over bare patches – water regularly in dry weather.

· Mow on dry days, if necessary.

Look out for...

- The first bulbs emerging and flowering: first snowdrops, then crocuses, daffodils and tulips.

- Birds taking twigs, grass and other materials to make nests.

- Caterpillars hatching and eating leaves – relocate them if necessary.

- Migrating birds arriving in the country after a winter away further south.

- Frogspawn and tadpoles emerging in ponds and lakes.

Garden fun

- Make a nature calendar: Observe which plants and trees put on their new leaves first and mark them down in a diary with the date/week of the year. Do they unfurl in the same order next year?

- Predict the season: An old country proverb says that if the oak tree puts on its leaves before the ash tree, summer will be dry and that summer will be wet if it's the other way round: 'Oak before ash, we're in for a splash; ash before oak we're in for a soak.' Keep a record of which tree comes into leaf first and the weather over summer. Is the saying true?

- Host the Snail Olympics: Draw a circle in chalk on a patio, then a larger circle around it. Find a snail each and carefully place it in the central circle. Use small stickers on their shells, if necessary, to mark them out from each other. Retreat a short distance to watch events unfold – the first snail to cross the line of the outer circle is the winner! Remove the stickers from their shells and put the snails back where they came from afterwards.

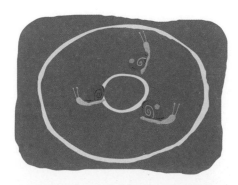

... Summer

Fruit, veg and herbs

- Keep the weeds under control.
- Protect ripening fruit and leafy crops from birds and butterflies, such as cabbage whites.
- Start harvesting.
- Re-sow some crops in early summer for a second harvest and/or continual supply, e.g. peas, dwarf French beans, carrots.
- Feed plants in pots regularly.
- Cut back herbs once they have finished flowering to avoid straggly, bare and woody stems.
- Pinch out any side shoots on tomatoes.
- Tie in climbing or tall plants regularly, but not too tight.
- Water regularly, especially plants in pots.
- Pot up strawberry runners.
- Carry out summer pruning on trained fruit trees and bushes.

Flowers

- Feed plants in pots regularly.
- Keep the weeds under control.
- Water regularly, especially plants in pots.
- Deadhead (remove old flower heads) from annual flowers and perennials that repeat-flower.
- Keep ponds topped up with rainwater, as required.

Trees and shrubs

- Prune flowering shrubs after they have flowered.
- Cut hedges – check carefully first for any birds nests and don't cut until after the chicks have flown the nest (if there are any).

Lawns

- Continue mowing.
- Water in very dry spells.

Look out for...

- Butterflies, bumblebees and honey bees collecting nectar and pollen from the flowers.
- Baby birds emerging from their nests, and broken shells on the ground.
- Dragon and damselflies hovering low over ponds and lakes.
- Baby frogs and toads emerging from the water to go and find a new home.
- Ants marching in line back to their nest.
- Wasps scraping wood from garden furniture with their mouths – they mix it with their saliva and spit it out to make their nests (a bit like papier mâché).

Garden fun

- Have a sunflower-growing competition: Whose gets the tallest?

- Enter your produce into a local village or horticultural show: There are often categories for flowers as well as fruit and vegetables, as you'll find lots of opportunities to get creative. You might win the longest bean competition, have the best plate of tomatoes or make the best animal from fruit and veg.

- Make a garden mandala: Use leaves, flowers, fallen fruit, twigs, pebbles or whatever is available to create a pattern or picture; the more intricate the better. Buddhist monks carry out this practice – it teaches patience in the creation, and the acceptance that nothing is permanent, as the mandala is slowly or quickly blown away once it is finished.

- Pest patrol: Check regularly for slugs, snails, caterpillars and aphids to prevent them ruining young crops and other plants. See pp61–63 for what to do about pests and diseases.

- Set up a garden play café or shop: Sell home-grown produce or mud and flower pies.

- Relax with a garden version of forest bathing: Lie under a tree and look up into the branches. Focus on all the sensations – look at the leaves and the sunlight dappling through them, the patterns that makes on the trunk; listen to the rustling of the leaves, the birds and buzzing insects; feel the ground beneath you and the grass tickling bare skin; smell the grass, trees and nearby flowers or herbs; feel the cooler air beneath the tree.

- Cloud-spotting: If there aren't any trees in your garden, do some cloud-spotting instead. Try to identify the different types of clouds, but also look for the shapes of objects in them – does that one look like a turtle, or is it a car?!

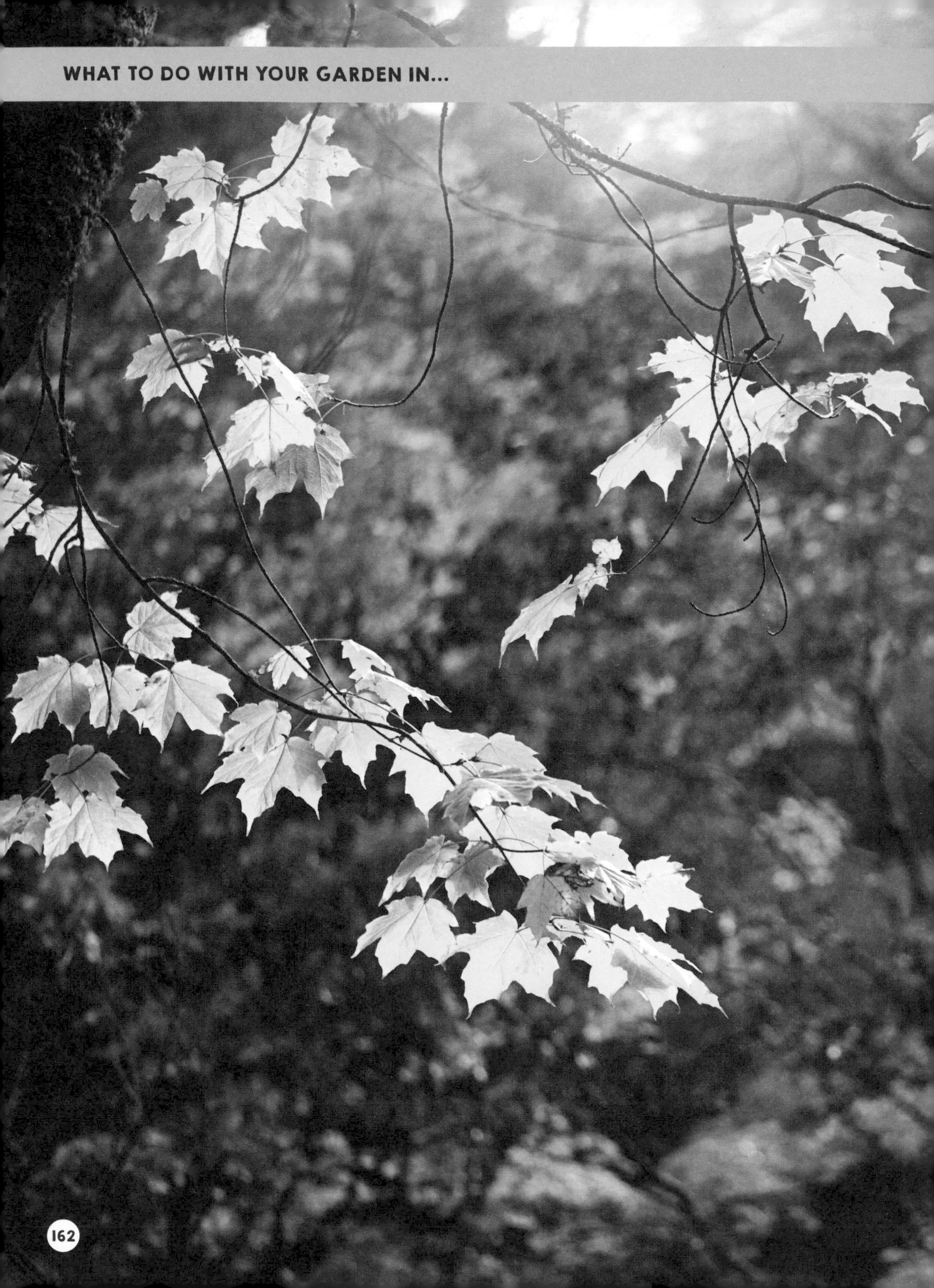

... Autumn

Fruit, veg and herbs

- Pick the last of the harvests; preserve and/or store anything that can't be eaten straight away.

- Clear away old foliage, plants and rotten fruit to avoid harbouring crop-specific pests and diseases over winter. Bean and pea plants can be cut off at the base and their roots left to rot into the soil – they will have fixed the nutrient nitrogen in the soil that will benefit next year's plants.

- Sow some green manure in bare patches of soil – these plants will grow, keeping weeds down until spring, then are chopped up and turned into the soil in late winter to feed it.

- Divide or move large clumps of herbaceous perennial herbs such as mint and lemon balm in early autumn. (Split the rootball of the plant with a sharp spade into two, three or four sections, removing all but one and backfilling the hole. The split-off sections can be planted elsewhere, or potted up to give away or bring indoors over winter, where they will give harvests for longer than they do outside.)

- Assess the successes and failures of the season, and make notes so that in spring there is a reminder of what to do more or less of the following year.

- Sow or plant overwintering vegetables such as garlic and broad beans. Look for 'autumn-sowing' on the packet label. These crops will give an earlier harvest than spring-sown ones, and garlic bulbs need a period of cold to divide into cloves.

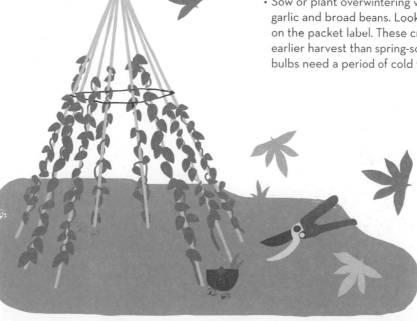

Trees and shrubs

• Rake up fallen leaves, especially where they fall on grass or over the top of shrubs/plants and/or ponds. A net over the surface of the pond can prevent most leaves falling into the water. Mix the fallen leaves into the compost heap or make leaf mould, a kind of home-made compost. Squash the leaves into old sacks or build cages from chicken wire and stakes and pile up the leaves inside. Allow them to rot down for two years for the best quality, although it can be used after a year as a mulch. The leaves rot faster if kept damp (water wire-held heaps in dry weather) and if they are chopped up into small pieces first (by a lawnmower).

Lawns

- Another chance to rake the old grass and moss out of the lawn if it needs it or it wasn't done in spring.

- Keep mowing until the grass slows down its growth and/or the ground gets too wet. Avoid mowing when the grass is wet to avoid spreading diseases and clogging the mower.

- Rake leaves off the grass (see above).

Flowers

- Clear away and compost foliage of dead annuals. Leave herbaceous perennial foliage standing where possible to provide homes for bugs and beetles over winter, and seeds in the seed heads for the birds.

- Save seed of favourite annuals and/or perennials (see p69).

- Edit the borders – did everything grow to its potential? Did the colour combinations work? Were there gaps? What could be changed to improve things next year? Make notes for spring, and move plants as necessary in early autumn (or wait until spring).

- Divide and/or move herbaceous perennials (see above) and plant new plants while the ground is still warm in early autumn.

- Plant bulbs for flowers in spring, such as daffodils, snowdrops, crocuses and tulips.

Garden fun

- Have a bonfire: Build the pile just before lighting it to be absolutely sure there is no wildlife sheltering under the twigs

- Throw a fire bowl party: Toast marshmallows on sticks and cook jacket potatoes (wrapped in foil) in the embers.

- Catch falling leaves for good luck: Superstition says to catch one leaf for every month to be lucky for the whole of the following year.

- Hang home-made bird feeders by smearing peanut butter into pine cones or threading an apple onto some string. Keep feeders topped up so the birds can rely on a regular food source.

Look out for...

- Birds leaving for warmer climates, especially geese in their v-shaped flying formations.

- The colours of autumn – which trees turn which colours?

- Shiny conkers among the horse chestnut leaves – thread onto string and hold a conkers championship.

- Hedgerow harvests of the last blackberries, sloes, haws, rosehips and nuts.

...Winter

Fruit, veg and herbs

- Raise pots off the ground on special pot 'feet' to help prevent them becoming waterlogged. Move pots of tender herbs into a more sheltered position or plunge them into the ground to insulate their roots against the cold.

- Prune fruit trees and bushes. For specialist guidance see the RHS website, or attend a fruit pruning course for first-hand practical advice.

- Order and plant bare-root trees and fruit bushes.

- Protect leafy winter crops from birds with secure netting.

- In late winter, visit a potato day event or garden centre to get seed potatoes for chitting.

- Late winter is also the time to sow chilli pepper seeds in a heated propagator.

Flowers

- Protect tender perennials and shrubs with horticultural fleece, straw, bubble wrap or by moving their pot under cover.

- Check supports (e.g. trellis, archways) are secure and strong enough to withstand the winter weather.

- Mulch beds and borders in late winter, and cut back any herbaceous perennials left standing.

Trees and shrubs

- Order and plant bare-root trees and bushes.

- Prune those trees and shrubs that need it.

Lawns

- Stop mowing once the grass is no longer growing, but keep raking off the leaves and any toadstools or mushrooms that appear.

- Avoid walking on the grass in very wet or frosty weather.

Garden fun

- Start planning for next spring and summer: What would you like to grow? Browse the seed catalogues for ideas. Why not make a mood board by cutting out or drawing pictures of your choices onto a large piece of paper or cardboard? This is a great way to plan out a garden.

- Wreath-making: Collect natural decorations for the holiday season such as pine cones, coloured stems of dogwood and willow, and evergreen foliage to weave into a wreath. Chillies, Brussels sprouts, feathers and seed heads or swag of foliage all make good additions.

- Decorate a tree outdoors: Use edible decorations for the birds.

- Seeing stars: Collect twigs around 30cm (12in) long and tie them together to make star shapes. Winter is also a great time to stargaze from the garden – which constellations can you spot?

- Play hide and seek or tag in the dark with torches: Shine the light on the person and they are tagged or found!

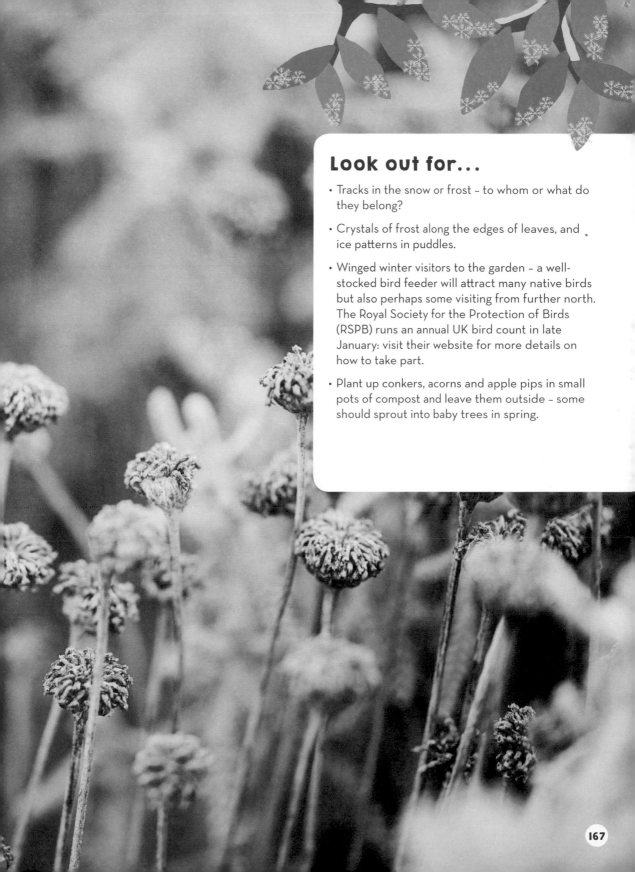

Look out for...

- Tracks in the snow or frost – to whom or what do they belong?

- Crystals of frost along the edges of leaves, and ice patterns in puddles.

- Winged winter visitors to the garden – a well-stocked bird feeder will attract many native birds but also perhaps some visiting from further north. The Royal Society for the Protection of Birds (RSPB) runs an annual UK bird count in late January: visit their website for more details on how to take part.

- Plant up conkers, acorns and apple pips in small pots of compost and leave them outside – some should sprout into baby trees in spring.

Experiment results and explanations

These results are what you should expect to see from the experiments, but if they have not turned out as expected or detailed here, investigate why that might be, perhaps repeating the experiment and changing one factor. Continual re-assessment and analysis form the basis of all scientific endeavours, and finding out what went wrong as well as right is a great way to encourage a young, enquiring mind.

Watch a seed begin to grow (pp32-33)

The seeds should germinate in a few days, and the warmer the spot the faster they will grow, so seeds kept inside should emerge faster than those kept outside. The root should emerge first, to help the seedling absorb more water to fuel its ongoing growth.

Cress heads (pp34-35)

The head in the most light should have the best growth. The one in the gloomy spot should have paler leaves and longer stems – the plants are trying to get the leaves higher in the hope that there will be more light further up. The head kept in the dark will still germinate, but the seedlings will have very little or no green on them, and will die once they have exhausted the energy stores in the seed.

Turn a white flower red (pp36-37)

By morning, the flower petals should be pink, or even red, depending on how much dye was used. The longer it is left the darker the colour will become, as the water evaporates from the petals but not the colouring.

Carrot top planting (pp38-39)

The carrot will sprout some small roots out of the side of the stub. Leaves – and maybe even a flower if it's left long enough – will grow from the centre. Unfortunately, it won't grow much of a new carrot, but the leaves are edible and can be substituted for some of the basil in home-made pesto!

Make a wormery (pp40-41)

The worms will gradually mix together all the layers into a single mass, and bring down the peelings from the top into the soil.

How much rain actually ends up in the pot? (pp56-59)

As little as a quarter of the water can fall into the bucket – the higher the pourer, the less it will be. If the pot also had a plant in it, even less water would have fallen into the pot as (depending on the size of the plant) the leaves can have an umbrella effect over the top of the pot, directing water away over the sides. Always feel the compost in pots outside to check if they need watering.

Glossary

ANNUAL A plant that grows from a seed, flowers, makes seeds and then dies within a year, usually between spring and summer. For example, sunflowers and nasturtiums.

BIENNIAL A plant that grows from a seed in one year, stays as just foliage (and root storage) over winter and then flowers the following year, before making seeds and dying. For example, foxgloves and carrots.

CHLOROPHYLL The chemical substance within a plant that enables photosynthesis to take place. It is green, and so gives the plants' leaves and stems their green colour.

COIR A product made from the fibrous husks of coconuts. It is sometimes used as a bulking agent and peat alternative in bought compost.

COMPOST The product of rotting down old plant material or other natural waste. It can be home-made or bought in sacks. Multipurpose compost is fine for most planting but there are specific mixes for plants that need more specialised care such as acid-loving (ericaceous) plants (e.g. blueberries) and cacti.

CUTTING BACK When a plant has all of its stems either shortened or cut back down to the ground, usually applied to the cutting down of herbaceous perennial stems that die back every autumn.

DECIDUOUS A plant that has leaves for only part of the year, growing them anew each spring and shedding them in autumn, often after they change colour. The pigments for the autumn colours are always within the leaves, and as the tree draws in the green chlorophyll along with other nutrients to store in the branches and roots over winter, the reds, oranges, purples and yellows are revealed.

DRILL A shallow trench made by scraping out the soil or depressing it with a stick or cane into which seeds are sown in a line.

EVERGREEN A plant that keeps its green leaves year round, such as many conifer trees and shrubs. There is a natural shedding of older leaves, usually in mid- to late spring, but the plant never loses all its leaves like a deciduous plant.

FERTILISER Plant food, providing them with the nutrients they need. Useful for potted plants.

FOLIAGE The leaves of a plant.

GERMINATION When a seed absorbs water, swells, then cracks open to grow a first root and shoot.

HARDY A plant that will withstand freezing temperatures. All AGM plants and all plants on the RHS database are given a hardiness rating, from H1a (needs constant temperature of 15°C or above) to H7 (will withstand temperatures of -20°C). Many other nurseries and garden centres also give indications of hardiness on the plant label.

HERB There are many definitions of what makes a herb, but here it is applied to plants that have a culinary or healing use.

HERBACEOUS PERENNIAL A plant whose foliage and flowers (all above-ground growth) die down over winter but regrow again in spring. For example, mint and geraniums.

MULCH A layer of compost, bark or wood chip, grit, gravel or other substance that is put over the soil. Mulch helps to prevent weed seedlings from growing, preserve soil water levels and, as it is taken into the soil over time by the worms, add nutrients and improve drainage in the soil itself. Apply once or twice a year to beds and borders.

ORGANIC MATTER Any rotted down plant or animal matter, such as compost or manure, that can be used as a mulch or soil improver.

PEAT A natural product cut/dug from boggy ground, peat is especially good at holding water so is ideal for using in compost mixes. However, it is a finite resource and also especially good at absorbing atmospheric carbon, so the horticultural industry is trying to reduce its use of peat and use alternative products instead.

PERENNIAL A plant that lives for three or more years. Those that only live for a few years are often termed 'short-lived perennials', others such as shrubs and trees can live for many tens or hundreds of years. Perennial plants can be woody or herbaceous (see Herbaceous perennial).

PHOTOSYNTHESIS The process by which plants make their own food using sunlight and water. See pp34–35.

PRUNING The considered shortening or removal of branches of shrubs or trees, carried out to promote flowering or fruiting and/or to shape and control the size of the plant.

ROOTBALL The roots of a plant and the soil/compost that surrounds them – everything that stays attached to the stem(s) when a plant is pulled out of a pot.

SEED LEAVES The first leaves that a seedling unfurls. These are actually held within the seed and pushed up into the light by the emerging shoot.

SEEDLING A young plant emerging from its seed, typically with a few sets of leaves.

SHRUB A woody, many-branched plant. Can be evergreen or deciduous.

TILTH The texture of the top layer of soil. For seed sowing, a fine, crumbly tilth is required.

TOPSOIL The layer of soil that is most fertile and sits on the top of the earth (below it is subsoil and so on, down to bed rock). For new gardens and raised beds, topsoil can be bought in small or tonne bags, or by the truckload.

TRANSPIRATION The process by which a plant loses water from its leaves, and in so doing pulls up more water through its roots from the soil.

TREE A single- or occasionally multi-stemmed woody plant. Trees are typically relatively slow-growing and attain the highest heights of all plants.

TRUE LEAVES The second pair of leaves grown by a seedling. These will resemble the adult leaves of the plant as it continues to grow.

WORMERY An artificial home for worms, used as a means of composting kitchen scraps, such as vegetable peelings.

Further resources

Hopefully this book will inspire your family to get growing. Here are some sources of further and more detailed information about gardens, plants, growing and garden wildlife.

The RHS

The RHS (Royal Horticultural Society) is the UK's leading horticultural charity, dedicated to helping everyone grow something. Membership allows for entry into its gardens and access to its experts – the advisory department can answer any gardening queries and it is possible to have your garden soil analysed by the Soil Department. The website (free to all) has a huge database of plants and their associated growing information, with many different search criteria, as well as advice on specific topics, such as making compost heaps and training/pruning fruit trees. Their flower shows have inspirational show gardens and lots of stalls at which to seek advice and new plants. rhs.org.uk

Other gardening organisations

Other gardening organisations that hold family events include Garden Organic (gardenorganic.org.uk), the National Trust (nationaltrust.org.uk), Chelsea Physic Garden (chelseaphysicgarden.co.uk), The Eden Project (edenproject.com) and the various botanic gardens around the UK. The National Garden Scheme (NGS) organises private gardens across the UK to open for charity – these can often be a source of ideas, information and interesting plants at the plant stall (ngs.org.uk). Other privately owned and charitable gardens also have events – look for local advertising.

Useful books, websites and plant nurseries

- *Creating a Forest Garden* by Martin Crawford (2010)

- *Plants from Pips* by Holly Farrell (2015)

- For more unusual fruits and herbs, try Otter Farm (otterfarm.co.uk) and Edulis (edulis.co.uk)

- For carnivorous plants, try Hampshire Carnivorous Plants (hantsflytrap.com)

- The RSPB (rspb.org.uk) has bird identification information and feeding advice

- The Wildlife Trust (wildlifetrusts.org) has local branches all over the UK and lots of advice on identifying and providing for garden wildlife

- Wormeries can be bought from Wiggly Wigglers (wigglywigglers.co.uk), who also have lots of advice on how to maintain them

- Plant identification resources include books such as *What's that Flower?* and the Collins guides to wildflowers, as well as *The Hillier Manual of Trees and Shrubs* and apps such as PlantSnap, PictureThis and Garden Answers.

- The RHS has information on green roofs on their website, or try Small Green Roofs (N. Dunnett et al, 2011) for a guide by the UK's leading green roof experts.

Index

A

accessibility
  raised beds 18–19
acid/alkaline scale 16, 20
air plants 144–5
allium 124–5
allotments 26–7
alpine plants 20
annual plants 17, 20, 120, 124–5, 127
aphids 61, 62, 161
apple 22, 96–7, 100–1
arum lily 28
autumn 127, 163–5

B

basil 76–7, 104–5, 114
beans, climbing 33, 72–3
bedding plants 17
beds 17
  raised 12, 18–19
bees 14, 32, 108, 128, 160
beetles 40
beetroot 39
begonia 142–3
biennial plants 39
birds 60–1, 62, 128–9, 130, 157, 159, 160, 165, 166
blackcurrant 92–3, 122
blight 62
bluebell 46
blueberry 20, 94–5
bonfires 165
borage 114
borders 17
broad beans 68–9
broken stems or branches 63
bulbs 20, 38, 124–5, 127, 154, 157
butterflies 62, 128, 159, 160
buying plants 48

C

cacti 24, 46, 136–9
carbon dioxide 34, 42
carnivorous plants 34, 56, 148–9
carrot 32, 39, 70–1, 159
cast iron plant 150
caterpillars 62, 128, 157, 161
celeriac 39
chamomile 106–7
cherry 98–9, 101
chilli 24, 82–3, 166
chives 114
chlorophyll 34
citrus trees 20, 28, 101
clay soils 14–15, 16
clematis 22
climate change 42
climbing plants 12, 22–3, 33, 50, 123, 146–7
coir 51
colour experiment 37
comfrey 59
community gardens 27
compost 16–17, 40–1, 51, 54, 61
conifers 127
containers 12, 20–1, 28
cornflower 120, 125
cosmos 124–5, 127
courgette 80
courtyards 28
cress heads 35
cuttings 113

D

daffodil 32, 38, 124, 125, 127
dahlia 125
deadheading 159
decorated pots and coasters 133
deforestation 42
digging 16–17, 50–1, 61
diseases 61–3, 163
drill sowing 52
dust 24

E

echinacea 121
ecosystem 42–3
ecosystems 61
energy storage 38–9
epiphytes 144–5

F

fennel 111, 114, 129
ferns 150
fertiliser 59, 61
flowers 32, 118–27, 159
  edible flowers 114–15
  plant theatre 127
  wigwam project 73
  wildflowers 14, 64
forest bathing 161
frogs 61, 130, 157, 160
frost 154, 166
fruit 22, 48, 87–101, 122, 154, 166

G

garlic, wild 114
ginger 24
grasses 127, 129, 133
green manure 59, 163
green roofs 22
ground cover 28
gunnera 28

H

hanging baskets 22
hedgehogs 61
herbaceous perennials 17, 48, 121, 124–5, 128, 165
  dividing 154, 163
herbs 20, 24, 103–17, 122, 159, 166
  herb seat 107
  herbal crown or wreath 109
  herbal teas 106, 111
hosta 46

05336480